FUNDAMENTALS OF
QUALITATIVE RESEARCH

JOHNNY SALDAÑA

FUNDAMENTALS OF QUALITATIVE RESEARCH

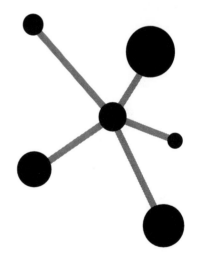

OXFORD
UNIVERSITY PRESS

OXFORD
UNIVERSITY PRESS

Oxford University Press, Inc., publishes works that further Oxford University's
objective of excellence in research, scholarship, and education.

Oxford New York
Auckland   Cape Town   Dar es Salaam   Hong Kong   Karachi
Kuala Lumpur   Madrid   Melbourne   Mexico City   Nairobi
New Delhi   Shanghai   Taipei   Toronto

With offices in
Argentina   Austria   Brazil   Chile   Czech Republic   France   Greece
Guatemala   Hungary   Italy   Japan   Poland   Portugal   Singapore
South Korea   Switzerland   Thailand   Turkey   Ukraine   Vietnam

Copyright © 2011 by Oxford University Press, Inc.

Published by Oxford University Press, Inc.
198 Madison Avenue, New York, New York 10016

www.oup.com

Oxford is a registered trademark of Oxford University Press, Inc.

Library of Congress Cataloging-in-Publication Data

Saldaña, Johnny.
Fundamentals of qualitative research / Johnny Saldaña.
p. cm.—(Understanding qualitative research)
Includes bibliographical references and index.
ISBN 978-0-19-973795-6 (pbk. : alk. paper)
1. Social sciences—Research. 2. Qualitative research. I. Title.
H62.S31857 2011
001.4'2—dc22   2010029012

Printed in the United States of America

ACKNOWLEDGMENTS

Thanks are extended to Patricia Leavy, series editor, for her gracious invitation to participate in this venture; the Oxford University Press production staff for their prepublication guidance; and my qualitative research professors and mentors: Tom Barone, Amira De la Garza, Mary Lee Smith, and Harry F. Wolcott.

CONTENTS

FUNDAMENTALS OF QUALITATIVE RESEARCH

1

GENRES, ELEMENTS, AND STYLES OF QUALITATIVE RESEARCH

THIS BOOK does not presume to serve as a comprehensive review of qualitative research but provides a practical introduction to its fundamentals, from this particular author's perspective. Qualitative research consists of an eclectic collection of approaches and methods used in several social science disciplines. *Fundamentals of Qualitative Research* first provides an overview of the field, then proceeds to its most commonly applied data collection methods. Research design and data analysis matters are discussed next, followed by recommendations for the writing and dissemination of reports, and resources for learning more about the subject.

Qualitative Research: A Definition

Qualitative research is an umbrella term for a wide variety of approaches to and methods for the study of natural social life. The information or data collected and analyzed is primarily (but not exclusively) nonquantitative in character, consisting of textual materials such as interview transcripts, fieldnotes, and documents, and/ or visual materials such as artifacts, photographs, video recordings, and Internet sites, that document human experiences about others and/or one's self in social action and reflexive states. The goals of qualitative research are also multiple, depending on the purpose of the particular project. Outcomes are most often composed of essential representations and presentations of salient findings from the analytic synthesis of data and can include: documentation of cultural observations, new insights and understandings about individual and social complexity, evaluation of the effectiveness of programs or policies, artistic renderings of human meanings, and/or the critique of existing social orders and the initiation of social justice. Qualitative research is conducted within and across multiple disciplines such as education, sociology, anthropology, psychology, communication, journalism, health care, social work, justice studies, business, and other related fields.

Just as there are multiple literary genres (short story, poetry, novel, drama, etc.), literary elements (symbolism, metaphor, alliteration, etc.), and literary styles (realism, comedy, tragedy, etc.), so too are there multiple genres, elements, and styles of qualitative research. Naturalistic inquiry remains solidly grounded in the non-fictional realm of social reality for its investigation, yet its write-ups can employ expressive and creative literary components.

Genres of Qualitative Research

A literary *genre* is a type or kind of literature characterized by a particular purpose, structure, content, length, or format. Different genres include poetry, short story, drama, novel, romance, and science fiction, for example. In qualitative research, there is also a variety of genre: the usual criteria are the particular approach to inquiry, and the representation and presentation of the study. The overview below is not an exhaustive list, but is a compilation of the most common genres in which researchers across multiple disciplines work. Also, some of these genres are not discrete; a few can be combined into one study. For example, an ethnography can also be a case study, an autoethnography can be presented in an arts-based research format, and so on.

Ethnography. Ethnography is the observation and documentation of social life in order to render an account of a group's culture.

Ethnography refers to both the process of long-term fieldwork and the final (most often) written product. Originally the method of anthropologists studying foreign peoples, ethnography is now multidisciplinary in its applications to explore cultures in classrooms, urban street settings, businesses and organizations, and even cyberspace.

Culture is a somewhat contested term and a difficult one to clarify—literally hundreds of definitions for the concept exist. Just a sampling of attempts includes the following:

> We define culture as: *knowledge* that is learned and shared and that people use to generate behavior and interpret experience. . . . [Culture is] social knowledge, not knowledge unique to an individual. (McCurdy, Spradley, & Shandy, 2005, pp. 5, 6)

But Chang (2008) offers an alternative to the notion of culture as a fixed and group construct:

> [P]eople are neither blind followers of a predefined set of social norms, cultural clones of their previous generations, nor copycats of their cultural contemporaries. Rather, . . . individuals have autonomy to interpret and alter cultural knowledge and skills acquired from others and to develop their own versions of culture while staying in touch with social expectations. (p. 16)

Thus, culture is not a "thing" but an individual and social evolutionary process. "Through the individual we come to understand the culture, and through the culture we come to understand the individual" (Sunstein & Chiseri-Strater, 2007, p. 286). But how does *culture* differ from and relate to the concept of *society*? Kendell (2004) explains:

> *Culture* is the knowledge, language, values, customs, and material objects that are passed from person to person and from one generation to the next in a human group or society.
>
> . . . [A] *society* is a large social grouping that occupies the same geographic territory and is subject to the same political authority and dominant cultural expectations.

> Whereas a society is composed of people, a culture is composed of ideas, behavior, and material possessions. Society and culture are interdependent; neither could exist without the other. (p. 42)

Of the many definitions and explanations of culture and society I've read, I've found that educational anthropologist Frederick Erickson's (1997) resonates the most with others since he cleverly uses a contemporary analogy to explain the term. Culture is like a "toolkit" that permits us to get things done. And,

> [by] analogy to computers, which are information tools, culture can be considered as the software—the coding systems for doing meaning and executing sequences of work—by which our human physiological and cognitive hardware is able to operate so that we can make sense and take action with others in daily life. Culture structures the "default" conditions of the everyday practices of being human. (p. 33)

The goal of ethnography, then, is to research the default conditions (and their "software updates") of a people's ways of living. For example, Rebekah Nathan's (2005) ethnography, *My Freshman Year*, reports a professor's observations of undergraduate life when she covertly enrolled as a full-time student and lived on campus. Her detailed fieldwork on student culture documents how a university's mission and goals do not necessarily harmonize with student cultural concerns such as dorm life, dining patterns, preferred friendships, and attitudes toward classes and scheduling.

Grounded Theory. Grounded theory (discussed further in Chapter 4) is a methodology for meticulously analyzing qualitative data in order to understand human processes and to construct theory—that is, theory grounded in the data or constructed "from the ground up." The originators of the methodology were Anselm L. Strauss and Barney G. Glaser, sociologists who in the 1960s studied illness and dying. Their original work has been reenvisioned by such later writers as Juliet Corbin, Adele E. Clarke, and Kathy Charmaz.

Grounded theory is an analytic process of constantly comparing small data units, primarily but not exclusively collected from interviews, through a series of cumulative coding cycles to achieve abstraction and a range of dimensions to the emergent categories' properties. Classic grounded theory works toward achieving a core or central category that conceptually represents what the study is all about. This core or central category becomes the foundation for generating a theory about the processes observed.

For example, Charmaz (2009) studied how serious chronic illness affects the body and the identity of self. A core category or "mode of living" with physical impairment that she identified from her interviews was *adapting*. Note how the word is a gerund (an "-ing" word) and implies *process*—actions that people take to solve a problem. Charmaz explains the theory, one that was not preapplied to the data, but one that emerged from them through her analysis of interview transcripts, appropriately coded to construct the actions at work in her participants:

> By adapting, I mean altering life and self to accommodate to physical losses and to reunify the body and self accordingly. Adapting implies that the individual acknowledges impairment and alters life and self in socially and personally acceptable ways. Bodily limits and social circumstances often force adapting to loss. Adapting shades into acceptance. Thus, ill people adapt when they try to accommodate and flow with the experience of illness. (p. 155)

Later in the narrative, Charmaz extends the analysis by outlining and discussing the stages people undergo as they adapt. Again, note the gerunds at work here: "After long years of ignoring, minimizing, struggling against, and reconciling themselves to illness, they adapt as they regain a sense of wholeness, of unity of body and self in the face of loss" (p. 156).

Grounded theory is a complex, multistage genre of qualitative research, but an approach that has been utilized in thousands of studies in many disciplines since it was first introduced.

Phenomenology. Phenomenology is the study of the nature and meaning of things—a phenomenon's essence and essentials that determine what it is. The genre's roots lie in philosophy's early hermeneutic analysis, or the interpretation of texts for core meanings. Today, phenomenology is most often a research approach that focuses on concepts, events, or the lived experiences of humans. The experience can be as mundane as grocery shopping, to as life changing as getting married. Motherhood, for example, is a phenomenon, and one of its essential elements is a parent with one or more children. But the purpose of this phenomenological study is not to examine the specific lives of, say, twenty mothers interviewed to gather data, but rather to synthesize the commonalities of their collective experiences and perceptions of motherhood. One essential that might be extracted from the data is motherhood as a "caretaking responsibility"; another essential might be motherhood as "protector of one's child."

Some qualitative research studies take a phenomenological approach when the purpose is to come to an intimate awareness and deep understanding of how humans experience something. It is revealing to another what goes through one's mind and what one feels as the phenomenon occurs. Some researchers will document these experiences thematically through such statements as "Motherhood is…" and "Motherhood means…". There are no specific methods for gathering data to develop a phenomenological analysis; interviews, participant observation, and even literary fiction, provide ample material for review. The primary task is researcher reflection on the data to capture the essence and essentials of the experience that make it what it is.

Case Study. A case study focuses on a single unit for analysis—one person, one group, one event, one organization, and so on. The genre serves as a reasonably manageable holistic project for novices to qualitative research to learn basic methods of fieldwork, data collection, and analysis. The purpose is not necessarily to develop an argument for how the single case represents or reflects comparable individuals or sites. Unlike studies that research a large number of settings or participants to gather a broader and more representative spectrum of perspectives, the case study in and of itself is valued as a unit that permits in-depth examination. Anthropologist Harry F. Wolcott addresses the most common criticism leveled at case study researchers when challenged with, "What can you learn by studying just one of anything?" His classic reply is, "All you can!" Nevertheless, any suggestion of the case study's generalizability or transferability is up to the researcher's logical and interpretive persuasiveness, and/or the reader's ability to draw inferences of how the case speaks to a broader population or issue.

A case may be chosen *deliberately* because of its unique character, thus presenting itself as a rich opportunity and exemplar for focused study—for example, a highly successful secondary school for adolescents of color in a lower-income neighborhood. At other times, a case may be chosen *strategically* because it is deemed to represent the most typical of its kind—for example, a moderately performing secondary school in a lower middle-class urban neighborhood; the ethnic distribution of its students parallels the ethnic demographics of the American population. Yet at other times, a case may be chosen simply and purposively for *convenience*— for example, a school in which the researcher's university has a collaborative partnership for preservice teacher education and field studies in child development.

Yet even within a single setting, there are diverse participants with diverse experiences and diverse perspectives. The "case" doesn't always refer to one person, and more than likely there is no single theme that perfectly captures how every individual within a group or organization thinks and feels. Nevertheless, in some qualitative studies, multiple cases might be examined simultaneously or consecutively for comparison and contrast. This approach places all cases in some type of context.

Michael V. Angrosino's (1994) classic case study article, "On the Bus with Vonnie Lee: Explorations in Life History and Metaphor," tells the poignant story of a developmentally disabled adult and his fascination and love for riding the city bus. Vonnie Lee's childhood was a troubled and abusive one, but as a young man entering the work force, he takes pride and joy in his new sense of independence and status. The article extends beyond the specific case by noting how the disabled do not have to be viewed as those with "disorders," but as individuals with lives as richly complex and metaphoric as someone from the average population.

Content Analysis. Content analysis is the systematic examination of texts and visuals (e.g., newspapers, magazines, speech transcripts), media (e.g., films, television episodes, Internet sites), and/or material culture (e.g., artifacts, commercial products) to analyze their prominent manifest and latent meanings. A *manifest* meaning is one that is surface and apparent—for example, describing a particular article of clothing as: a long-sleeved jacket constructed out of thick black leather with several silver-colored zippers and snaps, worn primarily for torso protection during motorcycle riding. A *latent* meaning is one that is suggestive, connotative, and subtextual—for example, that same black leather jacket symbolizing a member of "biker" culture and, when worn on a muscular, mesomorphic, bearded male, of a hypermasculine "outlaw" or "bad-ass" persona.

Some content analyses are both quantitative and qualitative in their design, since statistical frequency of occurrence becomes one important measure of salient themes, especially in texts and media. For example, the campaign speeches of two opposing political candidates may be analyzed by determining and counting the number of times each one says particular key words and phrases. The results may suggest not only what each individual candidate's platform emphasizes as a manifest reading of data, but also the latent messages suggested by their discourse when they are compared and contrasted with each other. One candidate's speeches may be imbued with frequently occurring words and phrases such as "community," "now," and "our responsibility," whereas the other candidate's speeches may highlight such text passages as "folks," "nation," and "back to better times."

Mixed Methods Research. Mixed methods research utilizes a strategic and purposeful combination of both qualitative *and* quantitative data collection and analysis for its studies. It is assumed that the epistemological (i.e., ways of knowing) and methodological advantages of each paradigm can work in concert to corroborate or more robustly support the findings, or to reveal complementary or even contradictory outcomes. For example, a group of participants might be administered a written survey that asks them to rate their attitudes toward a particular issue, such as their perceptions of their state government's effectiveness. A survey might include such response items as:

1 = STRONGLY AGREE 3 = DISAGREE	2 = AGREE 4 = STRONGLY DISAGREE			
I feel that at least one of my elected state representatives holds values similar to mine.	1	2	3	4
The state taxes I pay annually are a reasonable amount.	1	2	3	4
Our state governor is an effective leader.	1	2	3	4

Participants are instructed to circle one of the ratings in response to each statement. The mean or average rating is then calculated for each item. If demographic data are also provided by respondents, mean ratings can be compared by gender, ethnicity, age range, political party affiliation, and other variables of interest to discern any statistically significant differences in responses.

Then, a sampling of participants who took the survey might be individually interviewed to expand on the survey's prompts. "Our state governor is an effective leader" might initiate an interview question such as, "What are your perceptions of our state's governor?" The open-ended qualitative responses are then analyzed to determine if there is corroboration or contradiction with related quantitative survey responses.

Mixed methods research has been present for several decades, but only recently has the genre emerged as an approach that brings the once-separated quantitative and qualitative paradigms together to form a new epistemological, theoretical, and methodological way of working, when appropriate for the research purpose and questions.

Narrative Inquiry. Narrative inquiry is a research genre inclusive of a variety of approaches, but they share the goal of transforming data from, by, and/or about participants into literary story formats—an approach colloquially labeled "creative nonfiction." This genre acknowledges that humans tend to structure knowledge into narrative forms of cognition—in other words, we remember that which is in storied forms. If history were nothing but a bullet-pointed list of dates, names, places, and facts, it would be difficult to retain the information in our heads. But if there were a narrative that wove the facts to hold them together as a linear story line, we are more likely to make sense of history because we now have a plot that sequentially structures the details.

In everyday life, we also use story line and plotting as ways to make sense of current and past experiences. Our family lineage is a story, a student's university career is a story, even shopping for and purchasing an item of clothing is a story. There is a "What happens first, second, third,…?" and so on sequencing that keeps us on track with our daily routines, and "What happens next?" seems to be an almost universal curiosity hardwired into humans when we hear a story well told. Narrative inquiry recrafts the often scattered, improvisational ways we tend to share our accounts into well-plotted, artistic forms that utilize the conventions of fictional literature to present not just a more ordered rendering of life but an aesthetically rich one.

Tom Barone's (2001) *Touching Eternity: The Enduring Outcomes of Teaching*, reports the long-term effects of Don Forrister, an outstanding high school art teacher, on some of his students. As with most qualitative studies, Barone interviewed his participants to gather essential data, but rather than merely reporting and analyzing in an objective manner the teacher's methods and former students' reflections on how their mentor may have influenced their lives, Barone crafts his text with imagery and emotion to create an evocative, omniscient narrative reminiscent of literary short stories. In the passage below, one of the art teacher's former students, through Barone's interpretation, recalls a significant moment for her in high school:

> She had taken all of Don's classes, 3 years' worth, all of them wonderful and nurturing. She thought of his small, quick glances, his movements toward this student or that, the nods of affirmation, the laughs at students' self-deprecating remarks,

the clear-headed and not unkind criticism, the busyness of it all, but a business never devoid of compassion and joy. This particular incident had occurred during her first year with him, sophomore year, age of 15. Late afternoon. The class had been working on drawing still lifes. Hers had been a penciled rendition of a gnarled old tree on the river road, a tree that she had loved for its natural dignity. After seventh period everyone else had gone. She felt his presence. He had been looking at her drawing as she packed to go, had said to her at that moment, "You could be a good drawer."

Not "you are," not "if you worked hard," not the old cliché, "you have potential." Just "you could be a good drawer." Not gratuitous. Not meaning to flatter. Not cajoling. Not coercing. Just stating a positive fact.

To this very day, she remembered how flushed she had felt, in a glow, delighted that he had noticed her work, noticed her, intimating that her existence was valued, at least to him, to one who knew so much about things like what makes for good drawings. She recalled that it had taken her years to realize that it had not been a compliment, had been in fact much better than that. . . . From that point on, she had considered herself among the chosen. (Barone, 1997, pp. 228–229)

Poetic Inquiry. An emergent movement within qualitative research is the transformation of qualitative data or the expression of qualitative experience through poetic structures. Just as with literary poetry, the structures of poetic inquiry can take various forms. Sometimes a researcher will extract from an interview transcript the key verbatim words and phrases that seem to capture the essence of the text. The extracts might be kept in the same order as they appeared in the transcript, or rearranged or deconstructed for purposes of effect. An interview transcript sample from an older adult male might read (with selected words bolded since they seemed key at the time of transcription):

I **regret** not taking care of myself physically **when I was younger**. Now **my body**'s real **out of shape** and this **mass of**

fat and loose skin. I see all these **younger kids** and how **firm** and **toned** they are, and I think to myself **I could have looked like that** if only I hadn't eaten so much and exercised more. I'm **going to the gym** now just to lose weight, mostly, and so far I've been **disciplined** enough to go several times a week. I have this mantra that keeps me going, "Sometimes it's *not* about the journey—sometimes it's **about the** *destination*." I'd love to **lose about 50 pounds**, and if I give it time it's possible. There are all these **clothes** I'd love to buy and wear, but they only go so far up in size, you know? If I'm a **"large"** or, even better, a **"medium,"** I can **fit** into them.

The bolded words are then extracted, examined, and arranged into a poetic structure (sometimes referred to as "found poetry") to render an essentialized account of the participant's perceptions, though not everything bolded has to be incorporated into the poem, and minor additions can be added for clarity:

My body:
    out of shape
    a mass of fat and loose skin
Younger kids:
    firm
    toned
When I was younger, I could have looked like that
Regret. . . .
Going to the gym now:
    lose about 50 pounds
    large to medium
    disciplined
Sometimes it's *not* about the journey—sometimes it's about the *destination.*

Arts-Based Research. Arts-based research applies performing and visual arts media and methods to sometimes collect and most often represent and present its findings. Interestingly, not just academics but professionals within the arts industries have researched and interviewed key people for their products. Composer Steven Reich took selections from audio-recorded interviews with selected participants about trains in America and Europe during World War II and arranged their vocal rhythmic and inflection patterns into melodies for his musical work, *Different Trains.* Playwright

Doug Wright interviewed German celebrity and gay transvestite Charlotte von Mahlsdorf for his one-man Tony and Pulitzer Prize-winning Broadway play, *I Am My Own Wife*. In qualitative research, artistic modes of expression can be used to collect participant data. For example, children might be given disposable or digital cameras and asked to photograph their everyday worlds to gather data for the researcher on what is important to them. The photos then serve as stimuli for interviews with young people about the photographs' contents and meanings. The pictures can become part of the data display that accompanies a written article, or the photos themselves can be exhibited with accompanying written or oral narratives as an arts-based presentation for selected viewers.

As another example, adolescents of color might be asked to use their bodies to sculpt themselves and others into still images or tableaux that represent such abstract concepts as "discrimination," "prejudice," and "power." The facilitator may then ask them to move in space slowly in a way that shows how the body represents and transitions from "inequity" to "equity." This sculpting technique is called Image Theatre, a participant-centered modality based on the premise that we sometimes cannot put into words what we think and feel. These images are videotape-recorded as they occur, providing the researcher rich visual data to analyze and even play back to the participants themselves for a discussion of their own perceptions of the work.

It is sometimes difficult for some to understand how a ten-minute dance performance can be labeled "research" and its abstract movements "data," or how a hand-sewn quilt's patterns visually and symbolically represent the conceptual patterns of human action and feelings experienced during fieldwork. The arts are not just products, they are also epistemological processes—in other words, *ways of knowing through personal inquiry and aesthetic expression*. Art forms are media and rich metaphoric modes of communication that can provide insightful meaning when words alone are insufficient.

Autoethnography. Autoethnography is the reflexive, cultural reporting of self, most often through narrative. Davis and Ellis (2008) explain that the genre is "the study of a culture of which one is a part, integrated with one's relational and inward experiences. The author incorporates the 'I' into research and writing yet analyzes him- or herself as if studying an 'other'. . .". (p. 284). Though an individual's personal account certainly utilizes autobiographical details, autoethnography is more than just a retelling of one's life story or a key episode from it. Recall the various definitions of culture in "Ethnography" above. Autoethnography incorporates not just personal background experiences but personal ways of living and one's inherent value, attitude, and belief systems.

Lisa M. Tillmann-Healy's (1996) personal struggle with bulimia at various ages in "a culture of thinness" is graphically presented through a series of starkly written vignettes. This autoethnographic excerpt from a tale titled "Common Bathroom" suggests how rampant the problem is within university life:

> I chew the last Dorito and take a swig of Diet Coke. Without bothering to look up, I head down the hall.
>
> I stride to the common bath—the worst feature of dormitory living. When Gloria from the west wing exits, the swinging door nearly hits me in the face.
>
> "Sorry," she says with a smile. Her red eyes, filled with tears, give her away.
>
> "You OK?" I ask.
>
> "Never better," she responds, and I don't push.
>
> I move to the corner stall and lift the toilet seat. Fresh vomit sprays cover the rim.
>
> "You're getting indiscreet, Gloria," I say softly.
>
> I lean over and push my finger down my throat. The Doritos and Diet Coke come up stubbornly in thick clumps. "Bad idea," I scold myself.
>
> The swinging door opens again, so I pull my finger out, quietly put the seat back, and sit on the toilet, waiting. Someone enters the stall two down from me. She slides the lock into place. Instead of the expected bathroom sounds, I hear the toilet seat being lifted, then a flush. Over the whirl of suction, I can still make out gagging and splashing.
>
> . . . I am 19 years old. (pp. 93–94)

Some researchers take issue with autoethnography, asserting that the genre, if misused, can be nothing more than self-indulgent writing with little utility and transfer to the knowledge bases of a discipline. But autoethnography can also be perceived as a more authentic, first-person case study with rich details that provide a unique insider's perspective about the issues addressed. The genre also gives its writer intimate knowledge of what it takes for a participant to look inward to openly reveal personal experiences to others. A saying I pass along to others in my research classes is, "You can't learn how to tell someone else's story until you first learn how to tell your own."

Evaluation Research. Evaluation research systematically examines people, programs, organizations, and/or policies to assess their quality, merit, and effectiveness. The genre is customized to specific purposes and can employ a combination of both qualitative and quantitative data collection and analysis, when needed. Evaluation research is generally a contracted enterprise, and the best studies involve the immediate stakeholders as part of the evaluation process from the beginning, soliciting from them their perceptions of the program, and how the evaluation will ultimately help them redesign current and future endeavors. The researcher or research team doesn't necessarily assume an "objective" stance but assesses the values at work in case-specific projects, offering constructive and practical recommendations for improvement.

As an example, I was once hired by a state arts commission to evaluate one of their funded education projects in distance learning—that is, using cable television broadcasts of videotaped programming as a medium for the instructional delivery of classroom performing arts lessons to rural elementary schools. I interviewed the three production team members separately on their intended goals and perceptions of the project in progress and observed them at work during their rehearsals and studio tapings. But since I was a novice to distance learning, I also interviewed teachers and media specialists in the field to gain a better understanding of what makes for effective programming of this nature. Once the distance learning videotapes were completed, I previewed a thirty-minute episode to an average classroom of children (the project's targeted audience) and observed them as they watched the show to document their body language and verbal comments, which suggested interest or boredom. I then interviewed them as a group afterward and collected written survey data from them to further assess their responses to and engagement with the program.

The primary readers of my final evaluation report were two administrators of the state arts commission, but I also shared my observations and personal comments, plus the children's general reactions, to the production team members themselves. Aside from this specific case project, broader issues related to distance learning were also raised and evaluated. For example, one ironic finding was that the massively extensive number of clock hours the three-member production team devoted to planning, scripting, rehearsing, taping, and editing the television series could have been devoted instead to their live, in-class instruction directly for and with the targeted child audiences. In this particular project, distance learning technology did not effectively deliver the content to its constituents, as originally intended. Technology, in this particular case, actually lessened and inhibited the funded program's primary goal—quality arts instruction to rural children in remote areas of the state.

Action Research. Action research is conducted with the expressed purpose of not just observing social life, but reflecting on one's own practice or working collaboratively with participants to change their setting and circumstances for the better. Participants' lives and their social environment are examined critically. Diagnostics (via reflexive interviews, observation, journaling, and other data collection methods) are conducted to discern the specific problems and issues. Solutions and empowerment strategies are then implemented to initiate and hopefully sustain positive change. The researcher or research team serves as a facilitator of the project and, ideally, works equitably and democratically with participants since their personal investment, ownership, and stakes in the matter are more likely to generate significant outcomes. It is also possible to conduct an action research project for and by oneself, and the method is applied by such professionals as teachers to improve their classroom environment, and by clinicians to enhance their practice with clients.

One example of a participatory action research project is a community-based worker who observes that the adolescent Hispanic girls she counsels devalue themselves in overt and subconscious ways because of their gender and ethnic background. With the girls' permission, the adult worker facilitates with them a series of carefully designed workshops on gender and ethnic identity, accompanied with focus group discussions and introspective reflection through journaling and poetry writing. Most of the girls come to heightened identity awareness and a systematic understanding of social discrimination, and how sometimes their own actions reinforce and maintain their marginalized status. Under the adult facilitator's guidance, the participants develop strategies for self-empowerment and resilience, then "field test" these ideas in everyday social encounters, recording their progress in journals and through follow-up group discussion.

Investigative Journalism. Journalists and qualitative researchers rely on similar methods to gather data for their particular purposes: interviewing people, going into settings to witness events firsthand, searching for information in various archives and data banks, taking photographs, and so on. Journalists, however, target general public audiences for their work through news media and mainstream publications. And, a journalist's writing is not bound by some of the more discursive traditions and scholarly standards of academia, though investigative journalism can be just as rigorously conducted as ethnography.

This genre uncovers social life and most often reveals its injustices that are of current interest to the general public and policymakers. For example, Barbara Ehrenreich's (2001) *Nickel and Dimed: On (Not) Getting By in America,* reports her experiences with six minimum wage jobs. The purpose of the investigation was to work and live solely on this level of income for a period of time to learn if and how the sizeable population of people making minimum wage coped with it. Ehrenreich's honest and riveting narrative reveals the sometimes degrading and frustrating environments of selected workplaces, plus a meticulous account of the meager monies she earned and had to spend on basic necessities. Her final chapter presents an insightful analysis and critique of the economic and social conditions and issues she investigated.

Critical Inquiry. Critical inquiry is not so much a method as it is a social and political mission. Canella & Perez (2009) identify the critical inquirer as "a hybrid body that is researcher, cultural worker, investigative journalist, and activist/communicator for the public good" (p. 172). This genre is not just knee-jerk social commentary, but carefully researched issues that analyze and reveal social injustices. In many cases, the critical inquirers themselves have been part of the action or restoration efforts to work for change that will benefit the oppressed.

In the passage below, Giardina & Vaughan (2009) do not just recount but openly and unabashedly comment on the misguided and insensitive political motivations during the aftermath of Hurricane Katrina's 2005 destruction in the southern United States:

> In the days following Katrina, calls rang out from all corners of the country to "rebuild New Orleans." Congress author-ized an initial $50 billion in emergency funds. The American Red Cross pledged untold funds and dispersed hundreds of volunteers to the region. Even President Bush stated that New Orleans would be rebuilt "better than before." . . .

> *Better than before.* I supposed that is all a matter of perspective: Even from the outset, it was clear that if the powers-that-be were to have their own way, it certainly wasn't going to look much like the *old* New Orleans. Rep. Richard Baker [Republi-can-Louisiana] admitted as much when he told the *Wall Street Journal*, "We finally cleaned up public housing in New Orleans. We couldn't do it, but God did." . . . Of course, by "cleaned up public housing," Rep. Baker meant that he was thankful that the hurricane displaced those (largely poor, largely black) resi-dents who were living in impoverished dwellings, in effect making the now-abandoned or destroyed land prime for real estate (re)development. (p. 143)

Same Topic, Different Genres. Keep in mind that the same phenomenon, case, or process can be investigated using any one (or more) of the genres above. The specific genre selection, however, attributes expectations about how you approach the study and how its write-up may be shaped. For example, a broad topic for qualitative examination may be the seemingly mundane: "groceries."

An *ethnography* might involve spending several months observing the culture of one particular grocery store chain. A *grounded theory* study might explore the decision-making processes of customers "grocery shopping." A *phenomenology* could investigate with particular individuals what it means "to consume." A *case study* might focus on a soft drink deliveryman and his daily route and routines. A *content analysis* could be conducted to examine how cereal box art work may influence and affect potential buyers of the products. And a *mixed methods* study might investigate how the monetary costs and consumer-perceived qualities of "brand name," "in-store," and "generic" brands of packaged foods shape customer purchases.

A provocative *narrative inquiry* might render an omniscient stream-of-consciousness soliloquy as a woman thinks about what food items to buy while reflecting on her troubled marriage at home. *Poetic inquiry* could profile in elegant verse the delight of how a six-year-old child perceives the world of a grocery store. An *arts-based research* approach can document, dramatize, and per-form for an audience what workers actually talk about "backstage" in the grocery store's break room. An *autoethnography* might be composed by an undergraduate sociology student on her part-time work as a grocery store cashier to put herself through school. An *evaluation research project* can investigate why some grocery store chains succeed while others go into bankruptcy, while an *action research* project might explore how a homeless youth shelter could negotiate and collaborate with local grocery stores to receive food donations. *Investigative journalism* could explore a national food recall effort after an E. coli outbreak, while *critical inquiry* might focus on the contradictory excesses of junk food consump-tion and obesity amidst poverty and starvation in the country.

Just some of the qualitative research genres not discussed above are longitudinal qualitative inquiry, conversation analysis, discourse analysis, appreciative inquiry, oral history, and other specialized forms. But now that a broad landscape of a few major genres has been viewed, let's examine the constituent elements of inquiry.

Elements of Qualitative Research

In literature, *elements* are most often devices strategically employed by writers to achieve a certain effect. In Tennessee Williams' play

The Glass Menagerie, the unicorn glass figurine symbolizes the fragility and "oddity" of the disabled, painfully withdrawn character of Laura. In Dylan Thomas' famous poem about death, "Do Not Go Gentle into That Good Night," meter (referring to the stressed and unstressed patterns of syllabication) creates an ethereal and disjointed mood as one hears in iambic pentameter, "Do not go gentle into that good night.../Rage, rage against the dying of the light." Even nonliterary official documents have their elements, such as the use of organizational outlining (I. A. B. 1. a., etc.) and motif (e.g., the repetitive use of "Whereas" in a set of resolutions).

In qualitative research, as in literature, elements are devices strategically employed by writers to achieve a certain effect within selected genres. But elements also refer to what are elemental or necessary for a study to be conducted. These are not discrete components but things that work in unified concert, several with significant influence and affect on others.

The Researcher(s). An individual or team members, motivated by personal and scholarly interests, conduct a research study to investigate some facet of social life. The principal investigator initiates, plans, facilitates, and oversees all aspects of the project from start to finish, working in a rigorously curious and ethical manner to achieve the project's goals. The researcher, whether novice or veteran, is considered by many within the field of qualitative inquiry to be the primary *instrument* of the endeavor. Your autobiography and identity—life experiences, knowledge, training, emotions, values, attitudes, beliefs, gender, ethnicity, and so forth—influence and affect how you navigate through the enterprise and approach other important elements, such as the relationship between you and your participants and the analysis of your data. Who you are (or are becoming) determines to a large extent what and how you research.

Epistemology. Some refer to epistemology broadly as a theory of knowledge construction based on the researcher's worldview—how his or her lens on the world and ways of knowing it focus and filter the perception and interpretation of it. In contemporary research, some adhere to a *positivist* conception of truth as factual information that exists in the real world and thus can be reliably and validly documented with proper instrumentation and measurement. Others—most qualitative researchers, in fact—adopt a more postmodern perspective that promotes there is no absolute truth because it is contingent on context and multiple perspectives. Knowledge is *constructed* within the individual, rather than something outside of oneself waiting to be discovered. The goal is to come to insight and understanding about social life, not necessarily to predict and control it.

Such factors as your gender, age, ethnicity, sexual orientation, economic class, and so on, may not just subconsciously but even intentionally and politically frame your observations of the world. Women may adopt a feminist research epistemology to explore gender- and power-related issues. Lesbians, gays, and the transgendered may adopt the tenets of what is labeled *queer theory* in their study of gay culture, heterosexism, and homophobia. Researchers of color and their personal life experiences with prejudice and discrimination from the mainstream accumulate to develop a distinctive ethnic worldview. Thus, there are no such things as "neutral," "bias-free," or "objective" lenses for qualitative researchers. There are, however, guidelines and procedures available to enhance the credibility and trustworthiness of one's knowledge construction to develop a vivid and persuasive account for readers.

The Contextual Legacy. Research is situated in context. Our current projects build on the legacy of former researchers and their studies that have documented observations and analyses of social life. Methodologists have also provided recommended ways of conducting fieldwork and collecting and analyzing data. Theories exist for us to contemplate as frameworks for our research, or as challenges to critically evaluate and revise. A vast array of literature and media are available for us that shape our current studies, and we benefit greatly from our knowledge of and familiarity with those major works. Just as writers before us have contributed to the knowledge and practice bases of our disciplines, so too can we make active contributions through our substantive research efforts for contemporary and future readers and society at large.

The Purpose. The purpose of a study gives meaning, motivation, and direction to our work. The constituent elements of a purpose include the rationale or justification for the study, the topic, the central and related research questions and/or the problems addressed, and anticipated project outcomes. An umbrella term used for the overall epistemological, theoretical, and methodological approach to a study is called its *conceptual framework*. This template is not always fixed from beginning to end, for it can evolve and change as the research proceeds, as new insights into the study are gained, and as unanticipated contingencies occur.

Participants and/or Materials. Most qualitative studies will observe and interview people as part of their social investigation, but a few projects may rely solely on documents, artifacts, and/or media materials humans have created. To study the social world is, by default, to study humans and their products—complex endeavors to be certain. The people involved with our study are called participants, coresearchers, informants, and other labels, though the use of "subjects," still in use by some, is falling out of favor since it suggests a distant and overly clinical relationship. Participants' voluntary engagement in the project and our supportive rapport with them are necessary for the ethical conduct of research.

Ethics. Researchers, even those with action research or investigative journalism agendas, do not have complete free reign to do what is necessary to achieve their goals. There are moral and legal codes in place regarding the ethical treatment and care of people involved with research studies. The classic principle, "But first, do no harm," is the primary objective when working with human participants. Depending on your affiliation with universities, organizations, and/or governmental agencies, your study proposals are subject to review by established boards that oversee such matters to guarantee the safe design and ethical conduct of your work, especially with children and other vulnerable populations such as prisoners and pregnant women. Granted, there will always be subtle, slippery, even unsolvable dilemmas when we work with human participants because of unforeseen issues and the idiosyncratic nature of being human. For example, I once interviewed a seemingly upstanding young man about his future call to the ministry, only to learn through interviews that his past had been troubled with drug abuse and an alcoholic father, about whom he spoke disparagingly. I exercised my best judgment at the moment he disclosed these issues to listen sympathetically, but to not probe any further than we both wished to go. Thus, researchers need heightened attunement during all stages of a study to insure that no harm and minimal discomfort come to anyone.

Duration. All human endeavors, including qualitative research projects, are bounded by time. Some data collection stages may last only a few days (colloquially labeled "quick ethnography") due to restricted availability to site access, while other fieldwork projects in anthropology may last for decades within the same geographic area. The time we should spend in the field varies and depends on such factors as funding support, participant permissions, deadlines for study conclusion, human resources availability, and others. There is no standardized minimum number of clock hours required to assess a study's sufficiency and trustworthiness, but accounts tend to be more persuasive when the researcher logs an acceptable amount of time that others consider adequate for a study's purpose. For example, if we want to achieve the effect of credibly "being there" for the reader (its literary equivalent is called "local color"), then an extended period of months of fieldwork time with meticulously detailed fieldnotes may provide us with the experiences and data to write vividly and convincingly about the setting and its people.

The Field Site and/or Repository. Research happens somewhere, and the fieldwork locations of rooms, buildings, natural outdoor settings, towns, and so on, shape and are shaped by the humans who inhabit them. Even if we are not conducting participant observation in a specific social setting, there are sites where we must meet with and interview people, and they themselves may refer to their social settings and environments during the conversation. Cyberspace is not just a conceptual construct, but an actual entity, for digital data also requires tangible storage, transfer methods, electronic equipment, and sites for display. Even paper documents were produced by someone somewhere, and they are circulating in various locations or archived in selected spaces.

Within these sites are hundreds and often thousands of details that are part of human mental and physical extensions. Our entry into them is an opportunity to observe how space, environment, and objects reflect and affect the people within and around them.

Data and Their Collection. The Latin root of datum (the singular form of data) is "something given." As researchers we collect data as part of our study, but we must also remember that the humans we investigate give data to us as well. Some call the total body of data collected the *corpus,* suggesting that what we gather is not just a massive collection of information but a living entity to analyze. Data can be perceived as bits of information that range from one-sentence facts to paragraph descriptions about a setting to extensive passages of text revealing insightful awareness about the human condition. Grounded theory methodologist Barney G. Glaser is credited with the oft-quoted phrase, "All is data," meaning that anything that informs a study, be it interview transcripts or related fiction or the researcher's experiential knowledge base, has active contributions to make toward our understanding of a phenomenon.

Analytic Approaches. As data are both given and collected, researchers sort through these massive amounts of information to bring order and sense to them. Humans are pattern-making beings, and we apply that same process to data analysis. Patterns are constructed by reorganizing and grouping data into comparable categories and/or themes. But other genres of qualitative research approach analysis in more holistic, interpretive, and artistic manners. There are no standardized methods of data analysis for qualitative researchers, but there are several recommended ways for constructing meaning manually and with the assistance of technology. Though it is possible to offer our data corpus verbatim and unedited, we do a disservice to our audiences by not organizing and synthesizing the information into a streamlined, coherent presentation. If we wish to communicate to readers the core meanings of our study, we might utilize not only theoretical statements but even traditional literary devices such as imagery, metaphor, symbolism, and simile (e.g., "Teaching is like social work"; "Employees in the service- and helping professions engage in emotional labor"; "Culture is performance").

Representation and Presentation. The summary of a research study is presented in some type of appropriate form and venue such as a dissertation, journal article, Internet site, conference session presentation, stage, and so forth. The medium selected should be one that not only presents but best represents the story of the project. A ten-minute oral presentation of your work at a conference session may be soon forgotten by an audience unless an accompanying hard copy handout is provided for future reference. Access to your work increases when you publish in mainstream, high-impact journals. And if a dramatized adaptation of your research is formatted as a play script, the true test of a play's effectiveness is when it is mounted on stage as a reading or performance.

Selected genres of qualitative research also contain their unique elements (though they can most certainly be used across various studies). For example, classic grounded theory assumes that the researcher will identify a primary theoretical code or a central/core category that has been emergently developed through data analysis. A phenomenological study assumes that what will be reported are the essences and essentials of a phenomenon (e.g., what does it mean "to belong"?) in narrative or even propositional format. Mixed methods studies assume that both qualitative and quantitative data have been collected and analyzed and should be referenced in the final report. Even an arts-based research project about drawings participants created as part of data collection would feel seemingly incomplete unless photographs of some of their artwork were included in a written report.

Selected technical features of standard academic reportage are also elements and include such devices as the abstract, headings and subheadings, summary or conclusion, endnotes/footnotes, and references. Standard data display features such as tables, charts, matrices, graphs, flow diagrams, and other models are part of the researcher's canon of visual summary devices.

Elements of qualitative research refer not just to technical matters but also to *technique*. As a broad brushstroke conclusion, elements refer primarily to the *craft* of the endeavor.

Styles of Qualitative Research

Style is a somewhat elusive term, even in literature and the arts where it is most often deliberately pursued. To me, style is the interpreted, overall result of a writer's or artist's particularly chosen combination of genre and elements, integrated together to form a distinctive whole. The styles of qualitative research refer to the varied and available tones for its reportage and writing. If elements are the *craft* of qualitative research, then style is the *art* of it.

Styles also deal more with the *hows* of representation and presentation (most often in written formats) of a study's delivery to its audience. Genres, due to the nature of their approaches, address more of the methodological *whys* of the study, while elements deal more with the *whos, whats, whens,* and *wheres.*

Tales of the Field. John van Maanen's (1988) classic treatise, *Tales of the Field,* broadly classified types of ethnographic writing into several categories: realist, confessional, impressionist, critical, formal, literary, and jointly told tales. These are comparable to literary styles.

A *realist tale* is usually told in a third person/objective voice with a "measured, intellectual style that is uncontaminated by personal bias, political goals, or moral judgments. A studied neutrality characterizes the realist tale" (p. 47). Emphasis is placed on reporting the details of what participants say and do, followed by a rigorous analysis.

A *confessional tale* is a researcher's first-person, more intimate, "backstage" account of what transpired during the study. Biases, problems, ethical dilemmas, and emotional responses of the fieldworker are openly addressed when reporting the participants' stories. Ironically, these types of tales can be more believable than realist tales since "fieldwork is an interpretive act, not an observational or descriptive one" (p. 93).

An *impressionist tale* uses language's power of imagery, metaphors, and evocation to write about the more significant and dramatic moments of fieldwork. The reader "is asked to relive the tale with the fieldworker, not interpret or analyze it" (p. 103). Rich narration and stories provide insight into the participants' personalities and their "episodic, complex, and ambivalent realities" (p. 119).

Critical tales focus on the political and social ramifications of fieldwork, with a deliberate focus on the inequities and injustices of the world for achieving emancipatory goals. *Formal tales* emphasize theory derived from the systematic analysis of data. *Literary tales* emphasize the writer as storyteller utilizing the devices of realistic fiction to portray participants as "characters" in active story lines. *Jointly told tales* are collaborative, polyvocal constructions in which the researcher and researched share narrative space equitably in a coauthored account.

Description, Analysis, and Interpretation. Harry F. Wolcott (1994) identified three dimensions of qualitative research that may also function as styles: description, analysis, and interpretation. Though there is some overlap between these three and van Maanen's tales (including his later additions of *structural, poststructural,* and *advocacy* tales), Wolcott's dimensions are not just about the writing but how one gets there. Plus, the first dimension, description, builds a foundation for the latter two, analysis and interpretation.

Description remains firmly rooted in the data themselves to present a "factual" account of the fieldwork observations to answer the question, "What is going on here?" Ways of structuring descriptive accounts can include chronological documentation, a progressive focusing from the particular to the general, presenting a key incident or a reconstructed "day in the life" of the participants, and other ways.

Analysis presents a systematic expansion beyond description that identifies "key factors [in the data] and relationships among them" to explain how things work (pp. 10, 12). Findings are presented as a narrative or data display with an accompanying description of how they were achieved. Patterned regularities can be contextualized, compared with another case, and evaluated. The research procedures themselves are both spelled out and self-critiqued for their effectiveness.

Interpretation reaches out for "understanding or explanation" beyond the particular study to find broader application and meaning (p. 10). Sometimes the discussion can extend to relating the observations to established theory. At other times the researcher can reflect on how the study relates to his or her personal experiences. Alternative formats for the findings can be probed through interpretive means such as poetry and creative narrative. This aspect is the meaning- and sense-making dimension that addresses the higher-level question, "What is to be made of it all?" (p. 12)

Wolcott advises that all three dimensions can, but not must, be integrated into a single study, but description is the foundation on which analysis and interpretation rest. He succinctly summarizes the differences by stating, "When you emphasize description, you want your reader to see what you saw. When you emphasize analysis, you want your reader to know what you know. When you emphasize interpretation, you want your reader to understand what you think you yourself have understood" (1994, p. 412). The overarching goal is to not just transform data, but to transcend them.

Closure

Qualitative research is composed of a variety of genres, elements, and styles, and this introductory chapter reinforces that there is not one but many possible approaches to naturalistic inquiry. Generally, the investigative methods are eclectic, heuristic, and holistic, rather than prescribed, algorithmic, and linear. Emphasis is also placed on the researcher as human instrument, who develops not just rigorous skills but also empathetic understanding and personal creativity in the investigation and documentation of complex social life.

More on the genres, elements, and styles of qualitative research will be addressed as chapters proceed, but in the next chapter, the technical fundamentals of collecting qualitative research data are addressed.

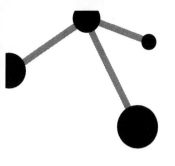

2

A SURVEY OF QUALITATIVE DATA COLLECTION METHODS

TO LIVE in the social world is to experience and reflect upon it daily. But to understand it deeply from a researcher's perspective requires that we collect sufficient evidence to document the patterns, categories, and meanings that humans have created. This documentation helps us to systematically and credibly examine, extract, and construct from the complexity of living its essences and essentials in order to exist in a better world. But there are also times when the complexities and ambiguities of being human are *exactly* what we need to document and report to contemplate the messy mysteries of it.

Some qualitative research studies may employ only one data collection method, such as interviewing participants, because the personal histories and worldviews of individuals will best answer the researcher's questions. Other studies will incorporate at least three different methods, such as interviews, participant observation, and written surveys, to gather a broader spectrum of evidence and perspectives to enhance the credibility and trustworthiness of an analysis. Other studies may not include interaction with participants at all, relying solely instead on the examination of documents, artifacts, and other material products humans have created.

During data collection, you'll certainly use several tools of the trade such as notepads and pens, laptop computers, digital voice recorders, and so on to document your fieldwork. But it is the researcher him- or herself who is generally regarded as the primary data collection instrument in qualitative research. Methods are not just seemingly mechanical techniques such as observing, writing, counting, and transcribing; methods also include your cognitive and affective processes such as inferring, intuiting, empathizing, and evaluating. These, too, can and should be documented because what you think, feel, and do during the entire research process are data as well.

This chapter surveys several data collection methods most often used by qualitative researchers. It is deliberately placed before the chapter on qualitative research design, first to acquaint you with the technical vocabulary of the field, and later to consider the methods' appropriateness for your particular project's purpose, research questions, and proposed representational and presentational forms. Also keep in mind that virtually all of the methods described in this chapter assume that you have secured any necessary institutional approvals and individual participant consent beforehand to conduct the study and collect the data (see Chapter 3).

Interviewing Participants

Many, if not most, qualitative research studies rely on interviews with participants. The data collection method is an effective way of soliciting and documenting, in their own words, an individual's or group's perspectives, feelings, opinions, values, attitudes, and beliefs about their personal experiences and social world, in addition to factual information about their lives. Your research topic, purpose, and questions form the basis for the subjects you cover and types of questions you ask during an interview, but the improvised conversation may also generate unexpected areas and insights for further inquiry.

Interview formats can range from highly structured, consisting of a set of prepared and specific questions to be asked in a particular order of each participant, to unstructured, consisting of nothing more than a general list of topics for possible exploration. Interviews can be prearranged but also happen spontaneously, such as when an opportunity arises to speak to a participant after you've observed her at work, and a span of ten minutes or so becomes available for a brief chat. Interviews can be conducted with just one person, several individuals separately, a couple, a family, or a larger number of people organized as a focus group. Depending on several factors, participants can be interviewed once or several times across the fieldwork period.

Selecting Participants to Interview

Determine which specific persons are appropriate for interviews and those most likely to provide substantive answers and responses to your inquiries. Of course, if your project is a case study of one particular individual, that selection is a given. But if your fieldwork is at a site where there are several people from which to choose, consider whose perspectives will best represent the diverse landscape of the social and cultural setting. For example, if your fieldwork is at a public school, individual interviews could be conducted with teachers and children from all grade levels, children's parents, the administrative staff (including the principal and secretaries), the service staff (such as janitors, cafeteria workers, and bus drivers), the school district's board members and superintendent, and others related in tangential to embedded ways to the setting's daily operations.

Of course, limited time, budget, and researcher energies will not enable you to interview everyone involved with the culture of schooling. Thus, *sampling*—the strategic, referred, random, and/or serendipitous selection of participants—will be used for relevant research purposes to collect a representatively broad to tightly focused overview of perspectives. If your research questions deal with a specific subset of a population, such as gender, ethnicity, age group, sexual orientation, occupation, status, or those with particular background experiences or histories, soliciting volunteers from among those cohorts is the obvious approach.

But how many participants are "enough" to find out what you want to learn? There are varying opinions on this. Studying the single individual case in depth makes for a rich profile, but the individual is not always representative of the population at large. Some studies have compared two diverse individuals separately to compare and contrast their perspectives. A small group of three to six people provides a broader spectrum of data for analysis, while others attest that, for selected methodologies, a minimum of ten to twenty participants is needed to insure more credible and trustworthy findings. Still others will recommend that you continuously interview people only until you're learning nothing new. At the opposite end of the spectrum, a large-scale project with a staff of research team members may interview hundreds of individuals across several years to assess longitudinal participant change. How many participants are "enough" can depend on many factors, but as long as you have sufficient interview data, whether from one person or twenty, you'll then have a sufficient corpus for analysis.

A caveat on convenience sampling: Some beginning qualitative researchers want to know if they can ask their friends to serve as participants in their projects. This request perhaps stems from the need to feel secure working on a new endeavor with people they already know and can easily access. But I do not recommend it. Depending on the topic, you may put your friends in awkward situations during interviews and observations. You might also make too many assumptions about what you feel you already know about your friends. And, you lose out on some valuable experience on what is takes to gain entry to a new site and to secure all necessary permissions and arrangements for fieldwork. The optimal choice is to research people you've never met before, or those with whom you're merely acquainted, and in specific locations and settings you have not visited or studied in depth. A famous ethnographic saying goes, "Make the strange familiar and the familiar strange," meaning that our goal is to come to new and intimate awareness and understanding about unfamiliar and taken-for-granted aspects of social life. Studying good friends you already know contributes little to your growth as a qualitative researcher.

Preparing for the Interview

Attend to the logistical matters of the preplanned interview. Contact or connect with your participant to negotiate an interview date, start and end time, and specific location—all at the participant's convenience. The day and time block should be one in which the participant will not feel fatigued or rushed, if possible. The specific location chosen should be free of noisy distractions, one that permits relative privacy to talk, and one that makes the participant feel comfortable and secure. If the space, such as a breakout room, needs to be scheduled with an administrator or facilities manager, the interviewer should attend to this detail and get some type of confirmation that the room is available and reserved for the date and time block. Contact your participant at least one day before the interview by phone and/or e-mail (if the participant has access to this technology) as a courtesy reminder, or to reschedule, if necessary, in case the participant needs to change the date, time, or location. Though not always necessary, it is sometimes useful to tell the participant ahead of time what will generally be covered at the interview.

Available time during interviews is most often limited, so every question asked should serve some purpose toward the research agenda. A first-time interview with a participant may go more smoothly if you develop a set of questions and prompts beforehand. Some methodologists have labeled this an *interview protocol*. The interview questions are most often different from the research questions but should derive from them to keep the study grounded. Generally, good interview questions solicit participant perspectives and stories. For example, if one of your study's research questions is: "What is the relationship between an individual and a pet?," some possible interview questions and prompts suggested by the research question might read:

- "What kind of pet do you have?"
- "Tell me about [pet's name]."
- "What is he/she like?"
- "What kinds of daily routines do you do with and for [pet's name]?"

Notice that "owning" a pet is a construct deliberately excluded from the questions, since "ownership" suggests a relationship that may not be held within the worldview of the participant. Prewriting some sample questions beforehand attunes you to careful language choices during the interview. These questions will hopefully generate responses that are inference laden—meaning that the answers provided by the participant clue you in as to how the individual perceives and takes care of his/her pet, and suggests a repertoire of particular values, attitudes, and beliefs. Of course, sometimes the best question to ask is the one you yourself are trying to answer. Thus, an interview question directly related to the research question might read:

- "How would you describe the relationship between you and [pet's name]?"

Preparing "I've heard" questions, strategically posed after the participant has given you her initial responses, enables you to compare your interviewee's perceptions with those of others:

- "I've heard that some people are 'cat people.' What is a 'cat person' to you?"
- "I've heard some people say, 'My pet is like my child.' What do you think of that?"

"What if" questions may also generate answers that provide more dimension to your research questions and solicit deeper perspectives from participants:

- "What would you do if, heaven forbid, your pet needed a thousand dollar operation to fix something that was wrong with it? What would determine whether you would spend that much on your pet?"

Three of the most common problems I've observed in novice interviewers are: constructing closed-ended questions, asking multiple questions as a single prompt, and asking either/or questions. A closed-ended question is one that potentially generates or requires nothing more than a one-word response. There are times when a simple "yes" or "no" is indeed appropriate as an answer, but there may be a tendency to ask too many of them in one sitting, expecting the respondent to automatically elaborate on the topic. An example of a closed-ended question is:

- "Do you take your dog regularly to a vet?"

Even though the respondent may answer "yes," this requires the researcher to ask a follow-up question. Transforming this into a more open-ended question or prompt is relatively simple and better guarantees a more elaborate response—that is, richer data:

- "Talk about your dog's health maintenance with your vet."

The second problem, asking too many questions at once, can overwhelm an interviewee. A cluster of related, yet too many, questions might read like this:

- "What kind of health care does your dog have? Is she pretty healthy most of the time? Does she have any kinds of recurring problems? Is she 'high maintenance'?"

If the questions have been prewritten in advance, this problem usually does not happen. Most often this issue occurs during the course of the interview when the researcher gets nervous and tries to make it easier for the respondent by improvising alternatives when, in fact, it only makes it worse. A more elegant initiating prompt might be, as noted above,

- "Talk about your dog's health maintenance with your vet."

Whatever responses the interviewee gives (number of visits per year, special health issues, etc.) can be followed up with improvised questions.

The third problem, asking either/or questions, may inadvertently set up the respondent with limited choices and may even inhibit genuine answers:

- "Do you take your dog to the vet regularly or only on an as-needed basis?"
- "Does your cat stay around you, or does he tend to keep to himself?"

Sometimes these either/or questions may be inadvertently preplanned or improvised during the course of the interview. Listening to and transcribing your recording of the event, which includes your own questions and responses, will attune you to any shaky questioning habits.

One recommendation to assess the quality of your prepared questions is to ask them out loud to yourself, then answer the question you just asked (assuming you have some background experiences with or knowledge of the topic). We write our questions on paper, but sometimes we do not voice out loud the possible answers we may receive. If possible, pilot test your interview protocol with someone not involved with the study.

For some interviews, it may be appropriate to use pictures or other items to stimulate participant response. For example, in my studies on how children respond to theatre after they see a play production, I show them a selected number of photographs of key moments from the performance as a way of assisting their recall and generating participant dialogue. In one of my interviews with teachers about newly written standards, I showed them the first few pages of an official state department of education document and asked them for their initial reactions. And for one of my longitudinal studies, I showed my case participant some artifacts (school materials, videoclips, etc.) from his past that I had saved for almost a decade and asked him what memories they evoked. If appropriate to your study, these visual and tactile prompts tend to stimulate rich response and can sometimes be more effective than questions alone.

If the interview is a second or third follow-up exchange from a previous interview, review the recordings and/or transcripts beforehand to formulate new questions or new topics for exploration suggested by the data. Something interesting you'd like to know more about, or something that was unclear the first time that needs elaboration, might also generate new and more specific follow-up questions.

Finally, before the interview, test your recording equipment to insure it works. Make certain you bring the equipment's power cord and/or extra batteries in case they're needed.

Documenting the Interview

Recent technology has made relatively inexpensive digital voice recorders available, though analog microcassette tape recorders are still in use by some. Digital recordings enable downloading onto computer hard drives or onto disks for later transcription and/or transfer into word processing or qualitative data analytic software (discussed later). Videorecording the interview can provide you with more nuances and inferences by analyzing the participant's facial expressions and body language. Videorecording small group interviews greatly assists the transcriber to determine who says what passage of conversation. Some participants, however, may feel extremely self-conscious with this equipment present during the process. I have found that voice recording most one-person interviews is sufficient for qualitative data collection purposes, while the documentation of small group interviews or focus groups, particularly with child and adolescent participants, is much easier with a digital videorecording.

Video- or audiorecorded interviews are eventually transformed into written transcripts and/or digitally downloaded into software programs to document and analyze the data. However, there may be those rare but occasional circumstances when capturing verbatim conversation is not possible. And, unfortunately, sometimes our best efforts to record an interview are waylaid by technological malfunctions. Thus, your written recollections and reconstructions of what was said become the data record. It is highly recommended that you bring to the interview a notepad and pen to jot down key words and phrases spoken by the participant, and personal notes and memos to self.

Conducting the Interview

There can be underlying and unspoken power dynamics between a researcher and a participant during the interview. Some of this stems from what might be perceived as an "expert" persona on the researcher's part and thus an enhanced status, while the participant might be perceived as an "expert" persona who has information the researcher wants and needs. Add to this the possible differences between the interviewer and interviewee's ages, genders, ethnicities, social classes, educational backgrounds, and so on, and power relationships and imbalances can potentially increase exponentially.

I advocate that the researcher always enter the interview with an attitude of courtesy and respect. The goal is to establish an atmosphere and working relationship of comfort, security, and equity. The participant is doing the researcher a great favor by giving of his or her time and experiences. I attempt to treat my interviewees, regardless of setting, as if they are important invited guests to my home. Also, in daily life we speak differently to particular people depending on our assumed roles and social contexts. How we speak to a parent is different from the way we speak to a best friend, to an employer, to our own children, and so on. We should also adopt appropriate tones with our participants. I consider all my interviewees as experts in what they know, but the way I interact with an adult participant is different from the way I interact with a child. As an older male in my mid-fifties, I can never have the same kind of interactions and relationship with a child participant as a twenty-five-year-old female might. So, I play a more "grandfatherly" role with youth rather than trying to "act like a kid."

The researcher is always a sympathetic and empathetic listener, someone who does not pass judgment on what the participant says, but one who provides a forum for a voice to be heard. Depending on the topic of the interview and the rapport and level of trust established, some participants may disclose honestly and unabashedly what they think and feel, or reveal questionable actions from their past. Others may wish to give a more favorable impression of self that nothing is wrong and everything is fine. Children in particular may offer to the researcher what they think is the "right answer" or what they think the interviewer wants to hear. Attune yourself to the nuances of voice and body language to discern whether participants are being truthful with their responses—not to challenge them directly, but to steer the course of your questioning to get at honest perceptions, opinions, feelings, and value systems.

On the date of the scheduled interview, arrive at the location with sufficient time before it starts to insure that the space is available. If necessary, rearrange any furnishings in the room, such as chairs and tables, to enable conversation. Bring bottles of water for both you and the participant in case anyone gets thirsty.

At the beginning of the interview, thank the participant for his or her time and willingness to be interviewed. Confirm the end time of the interview or how much time your participant can offer (which may be different from what the participant originally told you) and honor that end time or time limit. Proceed to any necessary permissions documents that may need to be reviewed and signed. Ask for permission to turn on the voice recorder and test it to insure that all's in working order.

In my first ethnographic project in a public school, I was "up front" with my teacher participant by stating that I was learning how to conduct research. The statements below were a deliberate attempt to bring her into the backstage knowledge of what I was doing. Though the transcript may read as if I were deliberately playing dumb, it was a sincere attempt to establish a sense of how the interview process works and to disestablish any misperceived power relationship:

> JOHNNY: I've been learning techniques of interviewing in my research methods class, and I'm supposed to describe the purpose and my agenda of the interview. And, so what I wanted to do was to talk about some of the things I've been observing that I kind of have questions about—like, for example, the speech tournament, and some of the assignments that you've been doing in classes. 'Cause, I've observed things but I don't know, for example, your reactions to some of the things like that.
> NANCY: OK.
> JOHNNY: The tape recorder can be turned off at any time when you feel you don't want anything on tape. And also, I'm supposed to be taking notes during the interview. I've never done that before, and I don't know what I'm supposed to jot down, but if you see me writing down something it's because something strikes me to ask you a little later and I don't want to forget...

I recommend that you, too, let the participant know the backstage operations of interview mechanics, and the purpose of your study. It demystifies the process and potentially creates a more equitable relationship.

If this is the first interview or early contact with your participant, and if there is a need to get any essential background information relevant to the study (such as his or her length of employment, educational background, current circumstances or conditions, and so on), take care of these matters at the beginning before proceeding into more in-depth or sensitive matters. The request for and sharing of basic information is a good warm-up for both parties before the heart of the interview.

Again, depending on the topic of your study, some interview questions will generate extended responses, while others will need a back-and-forth exchange with affirmations, questions, or prompting. In the excerpt below, the principal of an inner-city, lower-income, predominantly Hispanic school in the United States, talks to the interviewer (I) about her occasional substitute teaching for her staff, and one of the case study teachers, Nancy. All utterances from the audiorecording are included below to demonstrate the actual conversation that was exchanged. Notice the interviewer's brief responses throughout:

> PRINCIPAL: I think that teaching through games is important. You know, the reason there's joy here at the school is because I'm insisting on it—you know, that learning will be joyful. And I go into the drama class periodically and teach them some games.
> I: Uh-huh.
> PRINCIPAL: Um, I've been doing that because Nancy's been off-campus with the speech contest.
> I: Right.
> PRINCIPAL: And, you know, so I've been going and taking her class so that she could get some lunch or whatever.
> I: Oh, I didn't know that.
> PRINCIPAL: And I've been doing a game called "Detective" with the junior high kids. It's a mirroring game—you probably know it—you stand in the circle and, and you mirror and you try to, uh, get fast enough so nobody can tell who's the leader.
> I: Right.
> PRINCIPAL: And then you put someone in the middle who tries to detect the leader.
> I: That's fascinating, I didn't know that you would sub for those classes.
> PRINCIPAL: Oh, yeah, I sub for all the classes here. If a teacher is late or, um, needs to make an appointment or something like that, I'm normally available to do that.
> I: Do you do that just to, just out of your own heart?
> PRINCIPAL: I just do it because it just needs to be done. But, you know, I also use it as a way to show, the kids love to do that. Obviously there's a lot to be learned from mirroring and following directions and that kind of way. And I know a lot of theatre games. I ran, as I said, all those workshops for several years...
> I: Right.
> PRINCIPAL:... hired people, you know, monitored them, the whole bit.

It is not necessary for the researcher to provide continuous verbal utterances throughout the interview. In fact, it can become distracting for the participant if used excessively.

In the interview transcript excerpt below, Nancy, a second-year, grades K–8 White teacher in a predominantly Hispanic school in the United States, is being interviewed about her job. Like the interview excerpt above, notice how naturalistic, erratic speech patterns have been retained in the transcription. This question evoked an extended response that did not need interviewer intervention or probes:

> I: What kinds of things do you notice about this particular Hispanic population that's different from a White population, like the kind maybe you had at Johnson Junior High School [during your student teaching internship]?
> NANCY: Um, for the girls there's a lot more, there's a lot of pressure to conform, conform to, um, tradition, conform to what their *nana* or *tata* or mom or, you know, might think they should do to conform to be the girl that can have the *quinceañera*, you know? There's a lot of tradition, um, in their lives. And they want that, but yet they want it, you know, to be this modern type of teenager, woman, you know, going into womanhood. Um, and I see them struggle with that. I see them struggle with, especially, with especially the girls, like I think, struggling with wanting to succeed, but not wanting to be overly successful, if that makes any sense. They might be the first one and, and, they may have lived in here forever, but they might be the first one who've gotten through eighth grade, or who hasn't gotten pregnant before, you know, the age of 15. And, um, I don't know if that necessarily has to do with the different race, I don't think so, I remember, uh, it does in a way, um, I mean I know it does, but I remember some, you know, White kids at Johnson who, who were, you know, they were gonna be 15, they were ready to be pregnant too, you know? It's, it's, but it's, it does in a way, I know it does in a way, you know, have to do with this, with the tradition, and the way she'll differ there.

As the interview proceeds, take brief jottings to remind you of key words or phrases, or to write new questions and probes for follow-up. If the respondent raises interesting issues or insights that suggest further inquiry, these too can be noted for follow-up and probing ("Tell me some more about _____."). Avoid inserting your own extended commentary whenever possible; talk little and listen more.

Depending on the topic, or questions that may inadvertently trigger unanticipated responses, a few participants may ask whether they've sufficiently answered the question, venture into negative moods, or become emotionally distressed during the interview. Some of them may apologize for their reactions and try to quickly recover, while others may feel the need to continue talking about something important to them. As an interviewer, you may feel awkward with or uncomfortable about your participant's heightened states, but it is important to maintain and provide a sense of security. Do not ignore or discount the distress; provide encouragement and supportive comments that the feelings expressed are valid, that you appreciate the honesty, and that you are there to listen and not to judge.

At the end of the interview, thank the participant for his or her time but keep the voice recorder running. During the closure period, sometimes small-talk proceeds, and the participant may bring up additional thoughts worth documenting on the equipment.

Transcribing the Interview

If possible, immediately after the interview, listen to the voice recording from beginning to end to refresh yourself with the contents. Play the session on your way home or to your next task. If you are able to take some written notes as you listen, jot down anything that strikes you as an important passage, an insight that got made in your head, a connection to a larger issue, recommendations for follow-up questions, and so on. Also as soon as possible, back up the voice recording for security and begin transcribing the document.

Some researchers hire professional transcribers to transform the interview's audiorecording into a written text. If funding is available and time is a limited resource, employing these professionals to do the work for you is certainly an option. But by not transcribing an interview you yourself have conducted and will presumably analyze, you lose the opportunity to become intimately familiar with literally every word that was exchanged between you and the participant. Plus, transcribers may not accurately document the interview event, especially if the recording is of questionable quality. Some methodologists feel that the transcription process *is* analysis; others state that transcription is a vital warm-up for more in-depth analytic work. I propose that transcribing the interviews you yourself have conducted provides you with cognitive ownership of and potentially strong insights about your data.

Virtually everyone who has transcribed an interview comments on how tedious the task is. By the time this book comes to print, voice recognition software that is able to word process multiple voices on a single recording may be available to relieve some of the drudgery, but criticism has been levied toward technical accuracy. I now use voice recognition software calibrated to my own voice and speak aloud what my participant has said as I listen to the recording to get it automatically transcribed as a word processing file. I can always go back and correct any software errors that were made. Plus, the method is a way of taking even deeper ownership of the interview data by actually voicing what the participant himself said.

Depending on your research questions, goals, and experience, it is not necessary to transcribe the entire interview, just the highlights or what directly addresses your inquiry. I summarize the portions of the interview I am not transcribing verbatim to inform me of what the contents are in case I need to return to the original recording for additional data:

> I: What do you think were some of your reasons for the break-up with your first partner?
> LISA: His drug use was the biggest reason, especially since it was done behind my back, there was just no trust there...
> [LISA describes how one of her former colleagues got fired due to an inferred but unproven association with a drug user.]
> Anyway, yeah, so I just don't want any kind of relationship with a guy who's gonna be using drugs and wasting away his money on that kind of shit. It's bad news all the way around...

Transcribe the entire interview verbatim, of course, if you are conducting such genres as conversation or discourse analysis, which analyzes the detailed nuances of language.

It is also unnecessary to include informal or broken speech such as "uhs," "ums," and influent strings of speech such as "there was, uh, there was a kind of a, well, a, a," and so on, unless you need verbatim transcription detail, or feel the erratic speech patterns are inference laden. Use your jottings or the recording to note any special vocal dynamics by the participant such as significant pauses and word stress. Apply rich text features to portions of the transcript that stand out to you by italicizing, bolding, or highlighting salient words or passages. Use the conventions of dramatic literature's stage directions, which are placed in parentheses and in italics, for significant vocal cues, gestures, and body language:

> I: You said earlier that you felt there was nothing left for you in your last relationship, so you ended it. What was it that ended it?

LISA: Hmm. *(Extended pause; she looks sideways as she thinks.)* I think it started out OK but got worse, **much worse**, as it went on. Um *(moderate pause)*, I think I realized that it really wasn't what I wanted in a relationship, you know? *(Nods her head, looks back at me.)*

As transcripts are composed, insights and ideas for analytic follow-up may occur to you. Get these thoughts documented in analytic memos (see Chapter 4) or as footnotes or comments on the transcript itself. Interview transcript analysis will be discussed later. Now, the discussion turns to a second major method of data collection.

Participant Observation

Participant observation is a method whose legacy is rooted in the ethnographic research traditions of anthropological studies. Originally, fieldwork was conducted in foreign countries to observe and carefully document a people's culture—their patterns of living. Contemporary ethnography now takes place in urban and rural settings, school classrooms, business offices, major organizations, and cyberspace. The goal is to capture people's naturalistic actions, reactions, and interactions, and to infer their ways of thinking and feeling. Our written documentation of these human processes of what we say and do, traditionally labeled *fieldnotes*, is taken over an extended period of time to insure that we are present to witness the mundane, the typical, and the occasionally extraordinary events that compose human life. These researcher-constructed patterns of social action inform us in ways that we may be unable to gather solely from interviews or other data collection methods.

An interview can be an informative yet nonetheless artificial method of learning about an individual or a group of people. Participant observation is primarily the researcher's take on social action, whereas the interview is the participant's take. It is by watching people during their routines of daily living that we can supplement the data corpus with another way of knowing. What a participant says to us in an interview about his perspectives, and what we actually observe him doing in everyday life, may or may not corroborate. And what we observe as natural social action may intrigue but nevertheless puzzle us. So, participant observation can also function as a prelude to interviewing those we wish to speak with regarding what we saw and heard, and what we want to know more about.

Positionality in Participant Observation

Think of what it's like when you first arrive to a new place, such as a restaurant, university campus, city, country, and so on. Your senses may be a bit overwhelmed as they take in and interpret the unfamiliar surroundings. You move perhaps excitedly but hesitantly at first through the strange environment, unsure of where things are and the customary or expected ways of acting. You observe carefully to try to fit in, to look for what is familiar among the unfamiliar, and to not make any mistakes lest you appear foolish to others. Sometimes you'll talk to people who appear as if they belong there, asking questions of them in hopes of getting the information you want and need. One of them may be very friendly to you, and your initial inquiry may soon turn into an extended conversation in which you learn much more about the individual and the new setting. You may even discover that you have quite a bit in common. What you are doing is becoming acquainted with a culture. It may feel awkward at first, but after a few return visits or days in that place, your familiarity enables you to navigate more comfortably and confidently through the social setting, and to participate in it as would another member of the group already established in that environment.

This simulation is comparable to ethnographic fieldwork—the systematic, selective observation and documentation of participants' actions, reactions, and interactions in their natural social settings. Your research position within this process can vary, and your location (both physical and conceptual) may determine how much and what kinds of data you collect. There is a spectrum of researcher participation in a culture that he or she observes, ranging from an off-to-the-side, "fly on the wall" perspective, to being fully immersed in the daily activities alongside the people studied (Adler & Adler, 1987). The various positions along this continuum each have pros and cons for the qualitative researcher. A *peripheral* lens provides the investigator with a wide angle to assess the small details as well as the bigger picture, while documenting in written form the participants' actions as they occur. At the other end of the continuum, *complete* participation in the same ways of working and living as the culture under study provides the researcher with experiential knowledge that can more deeply enhance one's understandings of social life. Formal fieldnotes are not documented as life happens but in reflective "down time." Think of the difference between these two positions as comparable to sitting and watching a film as an audience member, to performing as an actor in the film itself. There is, of course, a midrange position in which participation in the culture's activities is *active* but selective, and not as immersed as someone totally embedded in the social group. The continuum available also suggests that your location and participation can vary from day to day, depending on the nature and site of the fieldwork, plus how the different positions can help address your research topic and questions.

Observing Social Life

Newcomers to fieldwork and fieldnote taking may feel overwhelmed at first, wondering what to document from the vast array of social details unfolding quickly before them. Acknowledge that you cannot possibly record everything, so as fieldwork progresses, shift your observational focus like a camera. On one day, observe the general scheme of things; on another day, focus on a particular space or a particular group of people; on another day, record solely what an intriguing individual case does and says; and on yet another day, survey the surrounding neighborhood or environment of the primary field site.

Also, you cannot document everything that happens in a social setting regardless of time spent in the field. There is a selective focus based on your research topic, research questions, or what emerges as salient in the participants' daily activities. The focus of your observations may also narrow as the study proceeds and a few issues rise to surface as core ideas for continued observation and documentation. Some methodologists have categorized what types of human patterns qualitative researchers might observe, but these are just recommended guidelines, not necessarily a fixed set of areas that must be observed. Gobo (2008) provides one such list of general areas for participant observation (and interview topics as well):

- behaviors, social relations, meetings, interactions, networks;
- situations and events;
- rules and social conventions;
- ceremonies and rituals;
- beliefs, attitudes, values, stereotypes, opinions;
- emotions, motivations;
- cultural products (such as pictures, paintings, movies, theatre plays, television programs);
- documents and texts (historical, literary, journalistic) (adapted from Gobo, 2008, p. 203)

The above list is a good array of effective categories for detailed observations. But since my personal epistemology is life as performance, I tend to look for three things in humans as character-participants in their social dramas: *action*, *reaction*, and *interaction*. Action refers not just to what individuals do but also what they say. Reaction is how an individual responds to what is said and done by others. And interaction refers to the reverberative nature of action and reaction in process—in other words, distinct units of action–reaction exchanges. (Theoretically, everything a person does and says is *both* an action *and* reaction. When my alarm clock beeps in the morning, my waking up is a reaction to the loud sound, but waking up is also an action unto itself. Most often one of these constructs—action or reaction—plays a more prominent role in what I observe in others and interpret.) My written fieldnotes do not necessarily divide or code life into these three distinct forms of social drama. The idea serves as a constant to attune myself to the intricate interconnectedness of people during their back-and-forth exchanges of talk, habits of listening, and bodies in motion—from subtle facial expressions to revealing gestures.

Most humans become leery, suspicious, nervous, and some even paranoid, when they are cognizant of being observed. Their feelings seem justified if there is a stranger sitting off to the side glancing at them occasionally and writing furiously on a notepad. Though researchers may claim to be observing "natural" social life as it is improvised before us, if our participants have granted us permission to be present in their spaces, actions may be changed to appear at one's best—such as what most people do when they knowingly are about to be photographed; we pose and try to look good for the camera. After a few days of observation, though, the novelty hopefully wears off, and what we observe about humans becomes more lifelike and genuine.

The Field Site

The classic retort to the question of what makes a successful restaurant is, "Location, location, location." The same might be said of what contributes to successful participant observation fieldwork. Location or the field site alone is not sufficient, but it is most certainly a critical component for gathering good data. For example, in the interview questions above about a person's relationship with his or her pet, it would be ideal to observe participants in actual exchanges with their animals. Observing how other humans interact with pets at such places as pet stores, animal shelters, veterinary clinics, public parks, and so on, in addition to private homes, better informs a study.

The topic and research questions of your project suggest the site or sites for your fieldwork. But this assumes that you have received permissions, when necessary, from key participants you will observe and/or the institutions at which they gather (e.g., a school, private home, business place, hospital, and so on). Observations at relatively private settings, such as a school classroom or health clinic, require permission from its administrative gatekeepers to conduct your research (e.g., a principal, a director of human subjects research). Generally, publicly accessible gathering places such as restaurants, stadiums, shopping malls, and so on, do not need permission from every person there, but you may still need your employing institution's Institutional Review Board approval to conduct the study and to observe in natural public social settings. (More on these permissions matters will be discussed in Chapter 3.)

Writing Fieldnotes

Initial fieldnotes are your written documentation of participant observation. They can be developed from live observation or extracted from a videorecording you've made on site. They are quickly composed, handwritten jottings of what your senses take in, how bodies move in space, and occasional rich quotes of what participants say.

Perspectives vary on how fieldnotes should be composed, and the methods described here are just one way to document social life in action. Write what you observe as descriptively as possible in the present tense, noting a select number of relevant details ("significant trivia," as I call them). Separate the "facts" from your personal inferences, comments, subjective responses, and interpretations of action by noting them in separate paragraphs labeled "OCs" or observer's comments (Bogdan & Biklen, 2007, pp. 163–164). Bogdan & Biklen also recommend titling each set of fieldnotes with a phrase that seems to capture the spirit of the observation.

Writing descriptively better assures that you are documenting social action, reaction, and interaction in a trustworthy manner for data analysis. The OCs are personal opportunities to render introspective meaning to what is observed. The subjective is certainly data, but subjectivity alone does not make a credible and trustworthy account of social life.

Below is an example of how the factual description of action is followed by related OCs. Participant observation takes place at a magnet school for the arts in an inner-city neighborhood in the United States. Note the descriptive documentation such as the day, date, location, and time frame:

Thursday, April 12, 2007, Martinez School, 1:00–1:30 p.m.: "Assembly Let-Down"

In the cafeteria, the custodian is still mopping up the floors while children are already seated around the perimeter of the space, leaving a large open square in the center of the room. Children are still entering through one of the double doors leading into the cafeteria. Available space on the floor is limited, and the seated children are asked to move up to provide more room.

OC: Ah, yes, school assemblies, I remember them well. I really didn't like them very much. It hurts to sit on a cold linoleum floor for a long time.

A junior high school–level class enters and one girl says to another, "Let's go sit over there, by the boys."

OC: Hormones! Assemblies seem like a great time to socialize in addition to being shuttled there for the "official purpose."

There is much talking at 1:15 p.m.—the scheduled time for a Native American dance presentation. The dancer is not present, and Mrs. Almanza, the dance teacher, is talking with a thin fifteen-year-old girl dressed in faded jeans and tight stretch top. The music teacher sets up speakers, microphones ("Test, test…"), and other sound equipment.

OC: So, where's the dancer? Pretty unprofessional role modeling to not be there since this is a performing arts magnet school. Calm down, he might have gotten stuck in traffic.

At a few minutes after 1:15 p.m., Mrs. Almanza takes the microphone and announces that the dancer is not here yet but "on his way." She introduces Pari, a former student of Martinez School, now attending Robeson High School in Valley City. The thin teenager takes the microphone and introduces herself as a Filipino who can sing "in English, Spanish, Mandarin," and her Filipino dialect.

OC: I'm impressed! I love the way they reinforced speaking multiple languages as an asset rather than a deficiency.

Pari says that she will be singing until the dancer arrives. Her first song, "Bambaleo," is in Spanish. The music teacher plays a cassette tape as she sings with a clear voice. She smiles and wiggles her hips in rhythm to the salsa-like music; smiles and slight laughter emanate from children. Halfway through the song, the audience claps to the beat. Two junior high boys sitting on a metal counter start doing a synchronized hand routine to the music.

OC: Where did they get that routine from? Is that some kind of music videochoreography? Some "in-thing" they know and do regularly? Check it out later.

The song ends and the audience—which is now almost every child and teacher at the school—applauds. The dancer has not yet arrived. Mrs. Almanza speaks into the microphone, "Thank you, Pari, that was fantastic!" She looks at the students and says, "Give her some more applause!" The students do so and cheer, whistle, and shout "Yay!"

OC: Well, if the resources you need are not there, you make do with what you have. This seems to be the ethic of living in this neighborhood. But it was a resourceful move.

OCs in the excerpt above were separated from the descriptive text, plus indented and italicized. Some researchers separate OCs further by assigning the passages a different colored font or highlighting the text in yellow on a word-processed page. Also note that direct quotes were placed in quotation marks. One of the most common errors of beginning field workers is neglecting to occasionally document what was *said* by the participants themselves.

After you've observed in the field for a few hours or the day, leave and find some private space to expand on what you've jotted, or to revise or add any particular details. This time can also be used to generate some initial analytic memos on what you saw and heard (see Chapter 4). Each session or day's handwritten fieldnotes should be transferred to a word-processed document and expanded further as soon as possible before the memories of the experience decay. Like interview transcription, several researchers note how tedious the task can be. But the opportunity exists to make new discoveries and insights about the data as they are written.

Taking fieldnotes on a laptop computer *as* you observe certainly makes the documentation and analytic processes easier and faster, and I recommend it highly when possible. But depending on the site, the sound of laptop keyboard "clicking" can be distracting for the participants. I have found it useful to occasionally video- and/ or audiorecord a session if the participants have given me permission to do so. The detail enables me to review it privately to supplement and elaborate on my written fieldnotes, to quote more precisely what participants said, and to document any exchanges of dialogue for more extensive analysis. Depending on the group observed, there will be an awkward breaking-in period with a videocamera in the space recording their actions and talk. Natural social action will be affected until the participants become accustomed to the device.

A fieldwork task that heightens your awareness of the participants' environment is drawing a diagram of the primary spaces in which you observe. Sketch a bird's-eye view of floor plans or outdoor environments, to scale as much as possible, noting such features of indoor spaces like doorway widths, number of windows (if any), and furnishings (see Figure 2.1 for a university weight room ground plan).

When possible, specify general clusters and foot traffic patterns of people within the space. Include in your fieldnotes supplemental descriptions on such features as ceiling height, quality of lighting, maintenance of the space, wall colors, and a general inventory of key artifacts. Occasional digital photographs of the field site and its participants also provide you with captured moments for more extensive observation and analysis of social details when they are embedded into your fieldnote document file. A more extensive set of fieldnotes in provided in Chapter 4 as an additional example.

Finally, always avoid passing judgment in the field. I recall years ago being observed as a novice teacher and seeing the note taker shake her head and make a loud dissatisfied sigh at something I said. Almost thirty years later, I cannot recall what I said in the classroom that provoked the reaction, but I will never forget her demoralizing response. If you have an issue with something you see or hear in the field, keep it private while observing and articulate your thoughts and feelings in your fieldnotes or an analytic memo. The exception to this, of course, is if you feel something needs your immediate action, such as children physically hurting each other, or a participant in emotional distress needing empathetic assistance.

Documents

Though contemporary social life has the moniker "the digital age," humans still produce and circulate astounding amounts of hard copy materials, depending on the physical site you study. These documents contain texts and images that reflect and metaphorically represent their creators' ideologies and value systems. A document's purpose can vary from the official to the commercial to the referential to the personal, and each one, if carefully studied

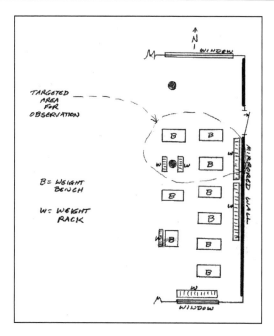

Figure 2.1. A pencil-sketch floor plan diagram of a university weight room.

and interpreted, suggests and reveals more than it contains at first glance.

At the field site, or in consultation with the participants you interview, look for and review any documents that are publicly accessible and, only with their permission, those archived in files, storage, or kept in personal spaces. Note the general contents of these items, where they were accessed, and, if there are many, keep a tally of the number of subtopics addressed. Log in your fieldnotes any particularly striking or inference-laden passages or images to you. When possible, keep a copy of key documents or scan them as part of your data corpus for future reference and analysis.

Below is a fieldnote example about the types of documents on display in a main office reception area of an inner-city school serving a predominantly lower-income Hispanic population in the United States. Note how the descriptive entry is accompanied with an "OC" afterward that reflects on the documents' contents, meanings, and their relationship to the particular site:

On a rack in the Family Resource Center are brochures and fliers, in both English and Spanish, about assistance programs available to students and their parents. The general school flier listed the services they provide: "food boxes, clothing, drug and gang prevention, volunteer neighborhood clean-up association, adult basic education, English as a Second Language classes."

Some of the surrounding agencies and organizations with their literature in the school racks include: Helping House, the United Way, the Metro South Community Mental Health Center, and the State Department of Economic Security's Family Assistance Administration. The government agency brochures list somewhat complex procedures, regulations, and requirements for assistance. Other types of services offered for families include immigration services and other social services such as domestic violence shelters. A statement from the immigration services brochure reads that the agency "assists those seeking to enter the mainstream of American life by providing… and by encouraging and maintaining cultural values and traditions."

OC: This lower-income school needs to deal with the realities of the people living in the "hood." Some of the teachers here call themselves "social workers," and the literature seems to support that, as you would probably never see a flier for food boxes and clothing publicly posted in a literature rack at an upper-middle class school office in this city. There you might see brochures for summer camps and enrichment programs.

I was struck by how complex the criteria and procedures were for getting governmental assistance. Why does it have to be so difficult to get help from public institutions that are in place to help its citizens in need? There may also be issues with literacy and the consequent frustration of trying to jump through all the red-tape hoops.

The secretarial staff of the school more than likely places the literature in the racks, but who initiates getting the brochures

to the school itself? The staff social worker? The principal? Are
they brought by the agencies themselves to this site? Talk to the
school staff to find out who decides what gets displayed.

Documents consist not only of previously produced materials but
also works created specifically for a study. Participants might be
asked to voluntarily maintain logs, journals, or diaries as a method
of gathering additional reflexive data. But this task can be burdensome on them, especially if they are busy professionals such as teachers or social workers. I recall reading several published research
reports that described the failure of participants to turn in anything
substantive when they were asked to keep supplemental records.
Some researchers are exploring how electronic messaging and online
social networking sites can make participant documentation easier
to get small units of spontaneous thoughts from participants.

Media Materials

Media materials data could be the sole focus of some qualitative
studies—for example, the content analysis of a collection of
Internet sites—or just one of several types of qualitative data gathered for a broader study—for example, an investigation of how
adolescents develop and maintain friendships through their secondary school years. The latter could collect data through individual and focus group interviews, participant observation at
schools and social functions, and samples of text messages and
e-mail sent to peers.

Digital culture has indeed produced new sources of data for
qualitative researchers. Internet sites, e-mail, instant/text messages,
chat room dialogue, tweets, blogs, vlogs, and other forms of media
communication produced or accessed by participants (assuming
they are able to) provide electronic footprints, traces, and signa-
tures. A participant who maintains a Facebook page, for example,
reveals an autobiographical portrait about him- or herself through
the text that's included and excluded, what visual images or links
appear, what group memberships are held, and so on. Text messages and tweets are small bites of output information that exhibit
initiated action and interactive reaction to human–digital input.

These forms of data are a bit more slippery to review unless the
participant voluntarily posts for open Internet access or directly

communicates with the researcher through these media. Collection and analysis of these materials are somewhat comparable to the processes for paper documents, but now there are electronic and digital contexts to consider. If, for example, the participant chooses to post personal musings through a video/vlog rather than a type-written blog, what does that say about the individual who feels that the visual broadcast of self is preferable to written text to be silently read by others? How often is text messaging conducted, and to whom? If chat rooms are visited, which themed rooms are they, and what do those themes say about the interests of the individual, particularly if a unique screen name and false online identity have been created? There are divergent opinions about the ethics of researching what is noncopyrighted and publicly posted online to virtually anyone. Debate continues as to whether such open acces-sibility requires the creator's permission to use his material for a study, or whether we can assume that public posting, by default, means free public access and use.

Virtually every researcher today relies on technology in one form or another to conduct the business of inquiry. Electronic media are no longer just tools, they are also the construction mate-rials of our work. As technology rapidly evolves and becomes more accessible to and integral with the general population's daily cul-ture, we should not consider it a given and therefore just part of everyday life, but a phenomenon that literally influences and affects modes of human communication and the quality of intra- and interpersonal relationships in virtual and hybrid spaces. As digital data from the field and from our participants are gathered, take special note of their sources, contents, and forms, for they are potentially rich and inference-laden units analyzed for their sig-nificance for the sender and receiver.

Material Culture

Participant observation focuses primarily on human action, reac-tion, and interaction yet will also document the objects and arti-facts that participants handle and that surround them within a field setting. A brief discussion of material cultural is warranted to insure that the researcher does not overlook an important and revealing component of social life and thus qualitative data.

Regardless of income, all humans possess or utilize material objects of various kinds for daily living (if not survival), occupation, and leisure. Whether the artifacts were made by the participant, given to her, or purchased and acquired by her, the possessions inform the researcher of what is important or part of her cultural world.

If we adopt a dramaturgical perspective that perceives life as performance, this suggests that we closely examine what "props" people use and own in their "settings." One of my female students conducting a case study with an adolescent girl held an interview, with parental permission, in the girl's bedroom. The interviewer was able to ask about various objects and posters that hung on the wall, prized mementos placed on a dresser, and even the décor. The items in the bedroom and its overall look seemed to reflect the young girl's personality, and the adult interviewing the teenager about her personal and semiprivate space was able to gain valuable insights on what was important and treasured. One adolescent student I observed pinned various buttons with political and social statements onto his backpack; two of them read, "Ask yourself questions" and "At first they burn books; eventually they burn people." I inferred from the messages on those buttons the student's social consciousness, value systems, and worldview.

Also, it is not only the objects within a space, but also the way they are stored and organized that can tell us much about the people who have primary responsibility for maintaining them. For example, I observed several teachers' classrooms at one particular elementary school. I noticed that the organization and appearance of the room reflected the individual teacher's management and instructional style. If the teacher was a firm disciplinarian with children, well organized with her curriculum, and clear and straightforward with her lectures, the clean and organized décor of the room reflected those same personal qualities. If the teacher was inconsistent with her disciplinary strategies, satisfactory yet unimaginative with her curriculum delivery, and a bit scattered in her lecture style, the disorganization of the room also reflected that "scatteredness." Teachers with warm and nurturing personalities maintained warm and nurturing physical spaces and décor. A very strict teacher who did not want children's desks moved for any reason maintained a linear, minimalist, and clean physical environment.

Since my background is theatre, one of my specialties is stage costuming—designing appropriate attire for characters from the world of the play. Costumers are taught to use line, color, texture, silhouette, and other visual elements strategically to suggest the character's personality to an audience. These artistic skills also create an attunement to real people's clothing choices and their connotations. I read and infer an individual's personality from such aspects of daily dress as the clothing's fit, colors and patterns, fabrics, designer labels, accessories, and so on. I assert that most people today have an intuitive "fashion literacy," and qualitative researchers can make some fairly astute observations about what people wear, why they wear what they do, and what their clothing choices reveal about them.

We needn't make a detailed inventory of each and every single object within the field setting or owned by the participant. We can infer a general "look" and "feel" suggested by the site, supported with a few fieldnote details about the furnishings, lighting, colors, cleanliness, and so on. We can also take a close-up and selected review of key objects and artifacts that seem to hold special meaning for the participants, or that strike the researcher as significant items within their social world.

Arts-Based Expression

Visual products created *by* participants can also be used as data. Artwork in the form of drawings, collages, and other media are extensions of the participant's self and ethos. Several research projects have reported successful outcomes with child and adult participants documenting what is important to them through photography or video of their everyday worlds. An interview with the participant about what she has created is essential to decode the artwork's subtle and hidden meanings, rather than interpreting the product on your own. Visual products can either enhance other types of data collected about the participant or serve as the primary data collection method when the participant is unable to contribute or the researcher is unable to collect substantive verbal data.

Another art form that generates significant data is improvisational drama, which may also include creative movement and other nonverbal modes of expression. Through dramatic simulation, participants place themselves in "what if" scenarios, using their bodies and voices to communicate what they may be unable to put into words, or what they may find easier to reveal using role play in fictional circumstances. Photographs and videorecordings of participants' dramatic work are helpful to more carefully analyze the dynamics and subtleties of dialogue, gesture, and movement, and the reflective processing of their own work afterward through group discussion.

Related Research Literature

Hopefully before and during the study, you've been reviewing the related literature in your field and topic of inquiry. Not only are previously published research reports useful as foundations and preparatory guidance (discussed further in Chapter 3), but they are also potential sources of data to support and enhance your analysis. Sometimes comparable studies can corroborate your own findings during fieldwork. At other times they may offer something different from what you've observed in your participants. But perhaps most important is the opportunity for your work to build on and expand the findings of others, or to approach a previously studied phenomenon from a new perspective.

The long-established literature review in academic research, with its entrenched status as an obligatory ritual or rite of passage for researchers, has been reconceived as an opportunity to collect a pool of preexisting data that not only influences the preparatory design of a study but one that also becomes an active part of a data corpus for analysis. Referring to and integrating the literature on an as-needed or as-appropriate basis into fieldnotes and analytic memos, as well as the final report, initiates connection with others' work, placing one's own research in nested contexts.

Quantitative Data

Qualitative researchers should not shy away from researching and including any statistical information relevant to their studies. This is not to suggest that mixed methods studies should always be the norm, but sometimes numbers can add insight, texture, and context to the repository of qualitative data in a report. For example,

Saunders (2008) reports on the dilemmas of United States citizens without accessible and affordable health care by first reviewing and contextualizing the numbers before the participants' stories are presented:

> The number of people without health insurance is HUGE—46.6 million.... That represents 15.9% of US residents—over one in seven. Let's try to imagine that number. It's greater than the populations of California, Missouri, and Alabama combined (U.S. Census, 2006). It would take over 900 major league baseball stadiums filled to the hilt to fit all of the people without health insurance. If every mile while going cross-country represented an uninsured person, you could travel over 7,000 times from California to New York round trip. (p. 529)

But statistics in a report do not always have to be sweeping in scope. The smaller numbers we deal with on a daily basis can provide points of reference for understanding different situations. Below, a Canadian health care worker relates the costs associated with meals at a nursing home for the elderly as she reflects on her coffee house purchase:

> I laugh out loud when I realize that what I've paid—$4.65 with tax, for my grande tazo chai crème, my Saturday after shopping treat—is 16 cents more than our per day resident food budget. Yeah, that's right—three meals a day, with a choice between two entrees at each meal in five different textures: regular, mince, puree, dental soft, and chopped. Plus, snacks with a beverage at 10:00, at 2:00, and before bed at 8:00. Plus, tea and cookies during the night for the wanderers. All that for $4.49 per resident per day. It's gone up 23 cents since 1993. Ten years and an increase in 23 cents per day per person. How much do you figure Starbucks has put up their prices in ten years? (McIntyre, 2009, n.p.)

As you conduct your fieldwork, attend not just to the qualities but devote some slices of time to the quantities of related matters—how many, how much, how often, how frequently, how infrequently, what increases, what decreases, and so on.

Managing Data

I advise the following as one method for maintaining the data corpus *for small-scale qualitative studies only*. Enter anything and everything that's related to your study in chronological order, as gathered, in one large word processing file. Multiple back-up files include the separate interview transcripts, separate fieldnotes, separate analytic memos, and so on, as a precautionary measure. But everything related to a single study is copied and kept in one large master file. I've found that this single document serves as my working corpus and helps me access and search for what I need faster than separate file maintenance. Rich text features such as bolding, italicizing, font sizing, coloring, and highlighting, plus the use of multiple headings and subheadings, assist me with at-a-glance retrieval as I scroll and search. The cut-and-paste function of word processing programs enables categorization of data into appropriate sections. For example, a fieldnote passage with a related interview excerpt and an analytic memo can be clustered together as a unit, and these separate units eventually join together into an appropriate sequence that becomes the skeletal outline and storyline of the study. The master document itself, through time, is eventually edited and transformed into the final report.

The final recommendations are to carefully protect your data by saving and backing-up your electronic files multiple times, keeping any hard copy materials safely filed with back-up copies stored in a separate location, and keeping your data private and confidential for ethical compliance. The research literature is occasionally peppered with stories of valuable, irreplaceable, and hard-earned data irretrievably lost due to technological failure, human error, and unexpected circumstances.

Closure

The data collection strategies reviewed above are only as good as their investigator. The quality of a qualitative study depends on both the information gathered and how it is analytically applied. The next chapter explores how these different methods might be configured and combined for a particular qualitative study's research design and consequent analysis.

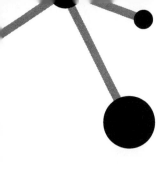

3

QUALITATIVE RESEARCH DESIGN

NOW THAT BASIC METHODS of data collection have been reviewed, their strategic employment for particular qualitative research studies can be described in context.

Before a longer work of literature such as a novel or play is written, an author will most likely brainstorm tentative ideas and outline the structure of the piece to provide better guidance for its development. Some will write out the story line or progressive action of the work that sketches what happens first, second, third, and so on, up to its climax and denouement. Others may write brief character biographies and descriptions beforehand that profile each person's major personality traits, values, likes and dislikes, and so on, in order to generate more appropriate, authentic, and motivated action and dialogue. Overall structures may also be developed, such as the division of major units of action into chapters, acts, or scenes, and how the story line and other elements fit into them. The latter is called *plotting* the literary work, and this is comparable to what qualitative researchers do when initially designing their studies. Literary writers always keep themselves open to moments of inspiration and revision as the creative spirit moves within them. Creativity, however, is not always a freewheeling process, but an openness to new ideas within a focused and disciplined work ethic. This is also the qualitative researcher's way of working when designing and executing the project.

Qualitative research design is best approached *provisionally* since this mode of inquiry is emergent and evolutionary in its process. Like many major tasks we undertake, we may plan beforehand for an event, but the unforeseen occurs and unique opportunities arise, so we need to be ready to change direction on an as-needed basis. Also, the description below seems as if designing a qualitative research study follows a linear progression of discrete steps, when in fact the major stages overlap, and each one has influence and affect on the others. Selecting the topic, conducting the literature review, composing the statement of purpose, and generating the major research questions, for example, are usually concurrent and reverberative rather than sequential activities.

Selecting the Topic

Generally, a researcher develops a specific topic or selects a particular problem for inquiry based on *disciplinary or social needs*, *pragmatic parameters*, and *personal passion*. But there is a gestation period in which multiple factors are considered before the final choice is made.

A review of the research literature in your field (see below) and in the areas that you are passionate about can give you some ideas of what has been accomplished to date, what topics need further investigation, and what specific problems or subtopics intrigue you. Several of my doctoral students say, quite rightly, that they wish to make a unique contribution to the field through their research. Authors of original research contributions generally have first reviewed the literature to survey what is already known, what is not known, what is suspect, and what can be synthesized and approached from new perspectives. However, a first-time, small-scale project to "cut your teeth" on qualitative research methods can replicate or investigate a facet of what's already been studied as a trial investigation.

Whom or what you wish to investigate can sometimes generate an idea for a study. Perhaps there is one particular individual that strikes you as someone worth knowing about because his or her practice is exceptional. Perhaps a group or site has a way of working or a culture that's considered unique or exemplary, and the reasons for its exceptionality are worth documenting. Another site, however, may seem problematic and in need of significant change, thus an examination of its issues merits a study.

The topic of your qualitative research project may be quite readily apparent for some, and a mystery for others. You may have several possible rich ideas for a study but still have difficulty selecting just one. One common pitfall for novice researchers is biting off more than they can chew—meaning, choosing a topic that is too broad in scope to complete within a reasonable amount of time. For a first-time project, propose your ideas to a mentor or instructor and get some feedback on the manageability of it. Discuss the feasibility within the pragmatic parameters of available time and expected product.

A few of the practical matters that limit the parameters of a study are: time, funding, and human resources. If your study is part of a class project, for example, the time limits of completion within a term set the boundary for you. If your project is an independent one that has some (or no) grant support, the resources of available equipment, personnel, and so on, have an effect. Plus, if you are the lone researcher and must attend to all details yourself, rather than a research team, that too determines the scope of the study.

Finally, your project must be something you yourself are passionate about. You will be devoting much to this endeavor, and the investment of time and mental and physical energy will seem more worthwhile if there is personal "payoff." But I do present one cautionary note: Be wary of using qualitative research as a forum for working out your own personal demons. This is not to discount the severity of a psychological issue, and writing about unresolved personal matters can be quite therapeutic. But I have read a few reports in which I inferred that the researcher's personal agenda drove and got in the way of the fieldwork. For example, some may be dealing with the death and loss of a loved one, or trying to resolve childhood abuse issues by studying and writing about others dealing with comparable matters. One can argue that researching what you yourself have experienced can make you somewhat "expert" at it. But if these personal pasts go unchecked or unclaimed from the start of your project to its final write-up, you may risk losing credibility and trustworthiness as a scholar. (The exception to this, of course, is if you are conducting an *auto*ethnography or writing experiential poetry, in which case your personal experiences *are* prominent and legitimate data.)

The Literature Review

There are diverse perspectives on whether a qualitative researcher should review the literature before a study. Some feel that you contaminate your openness to the forthcoming project by using others' concepts and theories, particularly purists of the grounded theory genre. But my primary recommendations for reviewing the related literature are to insure that you are basically knowledgeable about the topic, potentially making an original contribution to your field, and not reinventing the wheel. Certainly, you can address what others have already researched to corroborate the findings, to disconfirm them, or to find new perspectives on the topic. Regardless, you should have a basic literacy about the related issues of your project to inform your own research as you proceed. You may even discover new subtopics that hadn't occurred to you as possible areas for inquiry.

A mentor with knowledge about your field's literature can be an immense help in guiding you toward the primary works in your topic. But most likely you will be initiating your own search through the vast amounts of information in your discipline. The Internet has made searches and instant access a boon to researchers, but you won't find everything you need online. Get to a library to check what's in the stacks.

A note about keywords for searches: Each discipline's terminology has grown exponentially through time, and there can be multiple terms—sometimes fifty or more—that generally refer to the same broad topic. Autoethnography, for example, has also been labeled by various writers as: autobiology, ethnobiography, native ethnography, opportunistic research, personal experience narrative, and so on (Chang, 2008, pp. 47–48). Standardization is antithetical to qualitative research, but the freedom to develop one's own language use for methods or subject areas muddies the search waters. Take note during your literature review of the multiple terms and their definitions put forth by their specific creators for comparison and keyword entry.

First look for those monographs, journal articles, book chapters, and other sources that have already done literature reviews of some type. This is an effective way of getting a "grand tour" of a field and up to speed with the research in a subtopic. Works that are labeled *meta-syntheses*, *meta-summaries*, or *meta-ethnographies* of qualitative research have pooled related studies and profiled their key findings. Also check selected references listed in each piece of literature you review. Specific titles or recurring authors' names may provide you with additional leads to follow for more information.

When reviewing individual selections of related research literature, first read the summary content, if included: the abstract, concluding paragraphs, the final chapter, executive summary, and so forth—those portions that generally provide the overview of a particular study or subject. Being "front loaded" with the headlines gives you a more navigable journey through the entire work or informs you whether the work is irrelevant to your particular project.

Also, take careful documentation of the source's full bibliographic information for future citation and reference. If you accessed a book or journal from the library, include the item's call number in case you need to access it later. Note all information such as an author's full name and the city of a book's publishing company because the required format (MLA, APA, Chicago Manual of Style, etc.) for papers and articles will vary from field to field and from journal to journal. Also, document the full addresses of sites and pages you access on the Internet, along with the date you last visited them. Keeping this information in an Excel database will help you classify the materials as you continue your literature review, and the cells feature will enable you to type in key quotations or content summaries from each source.

Finally, if you have not taken a speed-reading course, I strongly recommend one from a reputable school or business. I took one as an undergraduate student, and it has significantly assisted my academic career. Speed-reading is not a just a set of methods but a retraining of your cognitive processes to quickly review and retain text in more time-efficient ways.

The Statement of Purpose

Anthropologist Harry F. Wolcott (2009) advises that writing a one-sentence statement of purpose for a qualitative research study is a tactic that focuses you on the central issue and direction of the project. It is the ultimate *why* that drives the study forward. The statement may seem or read as an obvious given, at first, but does require careful language choices to suggest or capture what the study is about, how it will be conducted, and what the projected outcomes may be.

For both the statement of purpose and its emergent research questions (discussed next), qualitative inquiry will most often address *how, what, in what ways,* and *why* social action happens and phenomena exist as they do. Some qualitative methodologists propose that asking *why* things happen is problematic because *why* assumes causation, a slippery concept to assert confidently in social science. Some even discourage asking interview participants *why* questions because it may lead to speculation rather than definitive answers. But I feel that qualitative researchers should not shy away from asking these types of questions because sometimes we do indeed want to know *why* things are as they are, not just the what's and how's. As long as we write a persuasive argument, documented and supported with sufficient evidence, we can at least attribute *probable cause,* not causation, to what we've observed. I myself no longer use the positivist construct of simple "cause and effect," preferring instead the multidimensional and multidirectional *influences and affects.*

The purpose statement is a single yet substantive and specific sentence that charges the researcher to investigate a facet or process of social life, and how participants or the phenomenon relate to it. Below are a few examples; note the researcher's role (to survey, to determine, to investigate, to explore), the modalities of inquiry (how, what, in what ways, why), and the specifically named participants or phenomenon:

- The purpose of this study is to survey how retail salespeople in "high-end" department stores respond to and interact with difficult customers.
- The purpose of this study is to determine what factors generally lead to small business longevity and financial success in Texas.
- The purpose of this study is to investigate in what ways undergraduate students of various majors initiate and maintain friendships through their university education.

- The purpose of this study is to explore why some Asian-American adolescent males in southern California become involved in gang subculture.

As you compose your purpose statement, experiment with various researcher charges (to identify, to outline, to describe, etc.) and the four recommended modalities of inquiry (how, what, in what ways, why) until you feel the most appropriate ones capture your intent.

The Central and Related Research Questions

If the statement of purpose addresses the *why* of a study, the research questions initiate the *who's*, *what's*, *when's*, *where's*, and *how's* of it. From the statement of purpose, compose a central research question and a series of related research ones. I offer that no more than three to five questions total should guide a small-scale study. The research questions might be developed before, during, or after the statement of purpose is formulated. Either way is fine, so long as the purpose and research questions harmonize with each other. Like all components of qualitative research design, even the research questions you formulate at the beginning stages of a project are provisional, as what you discover in the field may generate new questions, revise the original ones, and make some of them irrelevant.

Brainstorm a list of questions first, then organize them by topic. Explore which ones seem broader in scope, and which ones seem to flow from them. Some of the questions might also suffice as or lead to appropriate interview questions for participants. For example, one of the statements of purpose listed above was:

- The purpose of this study is to survey how retail salespeople in "high-end" department stores respond to and interact with difficult customers.

Research questions for qualitative research will generally lead to answers that describe, explain, or outline the story of a social *process*. Luttrell (2010) adds that research questions may also address the social *meanings* humans construct and attribute, the *contexts* of particular phenomena, and the *variances* that occur within them (p. 161).

A brief series of general research questions brainstormed from the above purpose statement might read:

- What makes a customer "difficult" to a retail salesperson?
- What factors (e.g., store policy, training, experience, personal judgment) determine how salespeople respond to and interact with difficult customers?
- What types of responses and interactions occur between retail salespeople and difficult customers?
- What are the expectations of customer service in "high-end" department stores as opposed to other types of stores?
- What is the ideal customer to a retail salesperson?

After the brainstorming, the questions are reordered, revised, or deleted as needed, then itemized into a central and related research question series:

- Central Research Question: What types of responses and interactions occur between retail salespeople and "difficult" customers?
- Related Research Questions:
  - What are the expectations of customer service in "high-end" department stores?
  - How does a retail salesperson define a "difficult" customer?
  - What factors (e.g., store policy, training, experience, personal judgment) determine how salespeople respond to and interact with difficult customers?

From the research questions, possible interview questions, foci for participant observation, and documents for review might be generated, all of which are intended to help answer the project's inquiries:

- Interview Question: "What are some examples or stories of difficult customers you've dealt with in the past?"
- Interview Question: "How might dealing with difficult customers influence and affect your perceptions of your job?"
- Participant Observation: The researcher shadows a salesperson participant and listens and watches his or her actions, reactions, and interactions with various customers throughout several business days.

- Document Review: Read the department store's employee or policies and procedures manual for any entries related to customer relations.

Notice how the provisional research questions now initiate other factors and decisions related to research design: the specific types of participants to be involved, the proposed field site locations, the choice of data collection methods, ethical issues to consider, and others. More on these matters are discussed below.

A brief discussion is merited on qualitative *field experiments*. Most qualitative research projects will study natural social life, while some empirical quantitative studies will administer some type of experimental treatment with participants to measure the outcomes. There are occasions, though, when a treatment of some type is provided to participants in a natural social setting, and qualitative data are gathered before, during, and/or after the experiment. This is perhaps most prominent in education, where an instructional method, the reception of content, or teacher–student interactions in an actual classroom can be observed. But rather than quantitatively measuring the outcomes, qualitative methods are used to gather participant perceptions of both the process and outcomes through interviews, observations, and/or written responses. If a field experiment or action research is conducted and documented qualitatively, the statement of purpose and research questions are constructed appropriately to reflect the nature of the treatment or action agenda:

- The purpose of this study is to observe how brain-based teaching and learning techniques influence and affect fourth-grade students' mastery of the language arts curriculum.
- Central Research Question: In what ways do brain-based teaching and learning techniques motivate fourth-grade students to attend to language arts instruction and enhance their knowledge and application of the content areas (e.g., reading, writing, speaking, listening)?

Participant and Site Selection

Chapter 2 described some of the factors to consider when determining the most appropriate participants and their number for a study, including the most appropriate field sites to observe them in social action, reaction, and interaction. Whether you're studying one individual, a small group, or a larger unit such as a school or organization, you will need to negotiate access to individuals and their space (discussed below).

As these matters relate to research design, the research topic, statement of purpose, and research questions developed thus far better suggest *who* and *how many* of them should participate. The *where* of the study is also implied as preliminary design matters for inquiry are solidified. For example, if we were to implement a study based on this statement of purpose,

- The purpose of this study is to investigate in what ways undergraduate students of various majors initiate and maintain friendships through their university education

we would first need to resolve who is represented as "undergraduate students of various majors." This could include thousands of individuals at one major university alone, and hundreds of thousands if we expand to other geographic locations. Thus, design decisions about sampling come into play. The same goes for field site selection: One university? Three? Five? Twenty? And in just one state or several across a region? How many is enough? If there were a virtually unlimited amount of personnel, funding, and time available to conduct such a study, the numbers and magnitude could be huge. But if this were a lone researcher project that needed to be completed within bounded parameters, it then would become not a matter of designing the schematics of participants and sites, but a matter of *redesigning the statement of purpose to better suit the scope of the study*.

This "teachable moment" illustrates the provisional nature of research design, and how revision of a study's preliminary matters are almost always necessary. Some visual designers first sketch their ideas for a formal artwork in pencil to experiment with ideas and layout. Drawing with a pencil also permits erasure if something committed to paper doesn't look or feel right. This same principle applies to qualitative research design. As your ideas for a study are "sketched" on paper, keep a mental eraser handy for deleting and revising its elements. Thus, the statement of purpose above, if conducted by one researcher within a limited time frame, might be restated to more realistically access available participants at a site:

- The purpose of this study is to investigate how a sample of female freshmen psychology majors at a major southwestern university initiate friendships during their first semester of study.

Note how the revised statement of purpose is now more specific and manageable in terms of who, how many, and where.

Data Collection and Data Analytic Methods

Data collection methods and their purposes were profiled in Chapter 2. As they relate to research design, specific choices are made based on which forms of data and thus methods to gather them will best address your statement of purpose and help answer your research questions. As for the specific data analytic methods to be employed, Chapter 4 will introduce you to several of them, but in a provisional research design, what you propose will be based primarily on the types of data you collect, and the genre of qualitative research you plan to adopt (e.g., ethnography, grounded theory, phenomenology, and so on). To some extent, at this point in the process, the writing *style* of qualitative research you choose (e.g., confessional, descriptive, interpretive, and so on) may also play a role in your selection of the data collection and analytic methods, but it will most likely be the other way around—the quality of the collection and analytic processes by you, the primary research instrument, will shape, to some degree, the style of the written qualitative report.

Interviews are the most common form of data gathering in qualitative research studies, perhaps because they directly solicit the perspectives of the people we wish to study. Ethnographic studies about a culture assume that long-term fieldwork and participant observation will be conducted to document social action. And if the statement of purpose and research questions relate to humans' relationship with technology, data such as Internet sites, e-mail, text messages, tweets, and other forms of electronic communication are the sources we must turn to and investigate. After your statement of purpose and research questions have been composed, review the repertoire of data collection methods to determine their appropriateness and utility for your specific inquiry. Ask yourself, what researcher actions—listening, talking, watching, reading, video taping, counting, and so on—will best help you gather the information that addresses what you want or need to know?

Another factor to consider in the research design is whether several and varied methods of data collection, rather than just one, are necessary for your particular study. Several exemplary qualitative research reports have relied solely on just interviews or just participant observation. But other exemplary studies have achieved that same status because they relied on and reported multiple types of data collected through various ways.

Multiple data gathering methods are purposefully chosen for several reasons. First, data gathered from different sources will better guarantee a spectrum of diverse perspectives for analysis and representation. If you want to study the phenomenon of motherhood, you could just interview women about what it means to be a mother. But you gain a deeper understanding of the topic if you conduct participant observation of mothers interacting with their children at home, on a playground, in restaurants, and other social settings. Even deeper understandings may occur if you read online social networking/support sites for mothers. These three forms of data, in combination, provide not only additional information but also additional *dimension* to the phenomenon.

Second, the limitations of one data-gathering method can be addressed by using an additional method. For example, participant observation is the researcher's lens and filter focused on social action, reaction, and interaction, but we can only infer what may be going through participants' minds as we watch and hear them. So, to compensate for this limitation of the data-gathering method, interviews with the people we observed can provide us with first-person accounts of what was and is going through their minds.

Third, multiple data-gathering methods (and sources) enhance the credibility and trustworthiness of a study through what is known in the field as *triangulation*—generally, the use of at least three different viewpoints. Interviewing children can give you an inside look at their world, but talking to both their teachers and their parents provides additional contexts for your analysis. Conducting a content analysis of newspaper articles about a particular social issue may be sufficient, but adding content analyses of television news broadcast transcripts and publicly accessible blogs from everyday citizens enriches the database. Just as we assess how many participants for a study are "enough," so too should we consider the sufficiency of one or several data collection methods for a particular project.

A final note about numbers: Quantitative research will concern itself with statistics such as frequencies and thus will include such phrases as "how many," "how much," "how often," "how constant," and so on, to describe its inquiry and consequent findings. Qualitative researchers needn't abandon numeric-based questions and data, for they can reveal interesting patterns of social action (e.g., asking a retail salesperson, "On average, what percentage of customers do you interact with daily that you would label 'difficult'?"). But counting should not be the central focus of a qualitative study; it should take a supporting role, not a leading one.

Representation and Presentation of the Project

The *representation* of a project refers to the best form and format that will credibly, vividly, and persuasively document the researcher's fieldwork experiences and findings. Such forms and formats (most often genres and styles of qualitative research) may consist of: a case study article, a confessional tale, critical inquiry, ethnography, poetry, narrative short story, and so on. The *presentation* of a project is the specific forum or venue for the research: a course term paper, academic journal article, conference session or poster presentation, thesis or dissertation, dedicated Internet site, YouTube video, DVD documentary, ethnotheatrical performance, published monograph, and so on.

The research design includes mention of the project's planned representation and presentation. But like all other aspects of qualitative inquiry, these too can change as the study proceeds. For example, I originally intended to write a standard thirty-page article about a case study for publication in an academic journal when, midway through the fieldwork, I serendipitously read a textbook on newer forms of documenting ethnographic studies, which included performance ethnography (Denzin, 1997). My conventional approach to published case study research transformed into a scripted one-act play for live theatrical performance because I discovered that the representation and presentation modes I originally chose were satisfactory but not the most appropriate for portraying the life story of my case participant—an aspiring actor.

The preliminary representation and presentation design choices for a qualitative project influence and affect other choices, but particularly the data collection and data analytic methods. For example, if you intentionally set out to conduct a grounded theory study (a genre of qualitative research), there are expectations within the academic community that your literature review has included and your presentation cites the work of such authors as Anselm L. Strauss, Barney G. Glaser, Juliet Corbin, and Kathy Charmaz. (Some may also expect citations of other grounded theory methodologists such as Adele E. Clarke, Janice Morse, and Ian Dey.) Though varied procedures for how to analyze data to develop grounded theory exist, even among its key writers, presentation of a grounded theory study will most often include: a description of the generally prescribed coding methods that were employed, descriptions of the major categories' properties and dimensions, an analytic narrative of participant processes, the central or core category, and, of course, the statement of the grounded theory itself.

Most researchers will enter a project knowing what genre of qualitative research (and its constituent elements) will be undertaken. The style, however, may be planned ahead of time but can unexpectedly shift, depending on what is discovered in the field or during data analysis and writing.

Project Outcomes

Though this may be difficult to formulate at the beginning of a study, especially if it is your first venture into qualitative research, consider what outcomes you would like to achieve. Obviously, one of the goals includes the formal presentation of your research. But this aspect of research design also refers to the more affective outcomes of all concerned.

First, consider how your participants may benefit from their involvement with the research. They should not be perceived as people in service to you, but as volunteers who willingly give of their time, space, knowledge, experiences, and—for some—their privacy, to better inform you of the human condition and the social world. Several qualitative researchers note how "talking through" the subject at hand can bring a better sense of awareness and even emotional catharsis for several participants after an interview. Their opportunity to be heard and valued for their perspectives may provide them with a sense of self-worth. Your personal acknowledgment of and gratitude for their contributions to both you and your academic discipline is important so that they do not feel used. Depending on the nature of the study, some participants may be paid a small amount of money for their time. A few methodologists object to this because they believe compensation somehow coerces expectations and thus skews the data. But I feel that underpaid working professionals and those with lower incomes who are part of a research study benefit if some type of token compensation— whether cash, gift cards, or in-kind services—is offered.

Second, consider how the potential audiences for your work may be affected. What do you hope the readers or viewers of your work will take from it? How can your research help a fellow researcher in the future who may also be interested in what you studied? How might your disciplinary field be enriched or even advance from your contribution? I genuinely feel I have become a better scholar by reading my students' reports, from term papers to dissertations. They acquaint me with research literature I have not had time to read and, through their documentation and data analysis, provide me with new understandings about participants and phenomena. The same goes for several published academic works and conference presentations by both novice and seasoned researchers. Scholars sometime wonder whether their work will have any effect whatsoever in the grand scheme of things, or whether it will simply lie unread on a bookshelf, in a journal, or in digital data storage. Yes, part of your legacy is your own responsibility—insuring that what you contribute is well written, substantive, and accessible. But we may never know how our research may influence just one particular reader's scholarship, or just one particular study's progress. I was once told by one of my mentors, "Just write what needs to be written, and the work will find its own audience."

Third, consider how you yourself as a researcher may change as a result of your investigation. Every study I've conducted has introduced me to new experiences and challenges in which I've improved my data collection and analytic skills. I've become better acquainted with the content and methods literature in several academic disciplines. I've been confronted with ethical dilemmas that forced me to examine my own values system as both a researcher and a human being. My action research project with children and bullying hopefully decreased one school's violence and made their classrooms better places to learn. I've become more aware and more understanding of social life in general and my personal self in particular. I've enhanced my curriculum vita and academic positioning through several key publications and conference presentations. And, I've met some wonderful participants and professional colleagues along the way. Whether the study you conduct is for an in-class term paper or for a full-length book, you *will* grow and change in positive ways after the experience.

Project Calendar and Schedule

Another difficult matter for newcomers to qualitative research is to estimate the amount of time necessary for a project from initial design through write-up. A folkloric piece of advice recommends that the number of days you devote to analyzing data should equal the number of days you spend in the field. Another piece of advice recommends that you write up a day's fieldnotes completely before venturing out into the field again. And yet another recommendation is that for every one hour of a recorded interview, you'll spend at least three hours transcribing it.

I cannot prescribe an exact number of clock hours or weeks you should devote to each of your project's stages since each enterprise is unique. But I *will* pass along this important cautionary note: It almost always takes longer than you think it will to complete what needs to be done. Forewarned with this, plan ahead. If you think you'll only need two weeks for fieldwork, plan on three or four. If you think you'll need just three hours to transcribe an interview, plan on four or five. If you think all you'll need to analyze your data is four weeks, plan on five or six. And if you think that nothing will go wrong during your study (such as a case study participant who enthusiastically volunteers to be interviewed, then suddenly withdraws due to her heavy work obligations), think again. *It almost always takes longer than you think it will to complete what needs to be done.* So, if available time for a project from beginning to end is limited, design the scope of the research study to what you can reasonably accomplish. But rest assured that once you gain more experience with qualitative research endeavors, the process goes a bit faster and you become much more accurate with your time estimates.

Work backward to plot your project's schedule. Log in a calendar the deadline or due date for the write-up of your report and go from there. I usually spend 15%–20% of my available time for research design and preparation, 50%–60% for fieldwork and data analysis, and 20%–25% for the final writing stage. These, of course, are just rough guidelines. And, consider that the write-up of the qualitative report actually begins during the research design stage, and the data analytic process continues through the write-up period. All necessary tasks for a qualitative research study are fluid through time. So, be prepared *and* be flexible. As much as possible, always stay ahead of schedule and never fall behind.

The Conceptual Framework

The conceptual framework (also known as a "theoretical framework" to some methodologists) is one of the most elusive processes of the qualitative research enterprise that many novices have difficulty grasping. It has been deliberately placed toward the end of this chapter because everything discussed thus far is part of it. In fact, it should have been the first element of research design discussed because all aspects about the qualitative research project flow from it. But to front-load this subtopic at the beginning may have made its explanation more confusing than helpful. So, now that you're acquainted with the more pragmatic and technical matters of research design, it's time to review the *epistemological, theoretical, and methodological premises* of them.

To use some colloquialisms as metaphors, the conceptual framework is more than the overall "game plan" or "modus operandi" for a research study; it's the *theoretical glue* that holds all of the preliminary design decisions together. Some use the image of a house's skeletal lumber framework as a way of thinking about the conceptual framework. The house's walls, roofing, doors, windows, and so on, are added as the research study progresses, resulting in a finished structure. But I like to use a different image for the idea of a conceptual framework. Think of a road as the research journey, and the *vehicle* you drive on it as the conceptual framework. The vehicle can range from a car to a truck to a van to a bus and can be one of various colors, years, makes, and models available. The overall type of vehicle you choose to drive on the research highway depends on several decisions you've made beforehand. Some of these decisions relate to research design matters (e.g., the statement of purpose, research questions, data collection methods, and so on). But also included as part of this vehicle—perhaps as its Global Positioning System or GPS navigation device—are the epistemological, theoretical, and methodological premises driving the overall research study.

Recall that epistemology is broadly conceived as a theory of knowledge construction based on the researcher's worldview—how his or her lens on the world and ways of knowing it focus and filter the perception and interpretation of it. If your researcher's lens sees women as an oppressed group with underrepresented voices in everyday life and in academic scholarship, then your epistemological premises are most likely feminist. If your researcher's lens sees social injustices in the world and you feel called or driven to improve its condition, then your epistemological premises are most likely critical or action oriented. Philosophical movements and frameworks are also epistemologies and include such terms as "constructivism," "pragmatism," "postcolonialism," and other conceptual ideas. It becomes even more complicated when you learn the multiple and hybrid combinations available to you, such as "critical feminist ethnography."

But at a more personal level, epistemological premises are also based on your own values, attitudes, and beliefs about the topic at hand. For example, if you feel or assume that most homeless adults have no one to blame but themselves for their life circumstances because they are unmotivated or irresponsible individuals, then your epistemological beliefs construct the phenomenon of homelessness differently than another researcher who feels that many become homeless due to inequitable social circumstances beyond their personal control. Sometimes we have to "see it to believe it," as the saying goes; yet sometimes, what we believe is only what we will see. But fieldwork experiences can radically alter a researcher's epistemological premises, including value, attitude, and belief systems, if he or she is open to discovery and change.

As for the theoretical premises driving your study, those will depend on your specific research topic. Theory will be discussed further in Chapter 4, but for now, a cursory and selective definition of a theory is: a statement with an accompanying narrative that explains how or why some things happen by proposing their most likely causes. Role theory, for example, puts forth that there are patterns of behavior and expectations associated with a position (Roberts, 2009, p. 240). If your role is a retail salesperson at a "high-end" department store, there are customer and employer expectations for your grooming, attire, speech, actions, decorum, and other aspects traditionally associated with the role. Other expectations exist for other occupational and social roles, such as doctors, politicians, students, parents, and so on.

Part of your research design preparation was to review the qualitative literature in your field. If you've done a sufficient job exploring the scholarly legacy, you will hopefully have noticed how other researchers framed their own work with selected relevant theories. Their goal was not necessarily to corroborate or disprove the theories they cited, or to reinvent the wheel by conducting yet another study that seemed generated by the theories they referenced. The theories they cited as part of their conceptual frameworks (whether they labeled them as such or not) were helpful directions for their journeys. If you want to refer back to the vehicle metaphor, think of theory as part of the GPS device that voices aloud to you, "Turn right," "Proceed forward," "Stop ahead," and other specific navigational prompts. You're driving to a specific destination, and the GPS device as theory *guides* and *advises* you along the way as to how to get there.

Remember the research study profiled above of the ways retail salespeople deal with difficult customers? What theories are involved with these types of interactions? There are several well-established ones from which to choose. Some of these theories deal with *role, power, social class, status, positioning,* and *negotiating,* to name a few. A researcher interested in salesperson–customer relationships would explore not only the actual exchanges observed or talked about, but also the *conceptual* dynamics at work.

As an extended example, one of my ethnographic studies observed a beginning teacher over the first twenty months of her professional career. She was a White, middle-class woman teaching in a U.S. school with a lower-class Hispanic population. The first two years of her practice were a rocky journey as she dealt with issues she had not encountered in her past, such as poverty, gangs, and non–English speaking children. Her story in and of itself was an intriguing one, but there was no glue that held it all together. "Culture" was a major concept at work in this field site, but the concept was too broad to have any analytic utility for me—in other words, what *isn't* cultural in one way or another?

Midway through the study as I continued to review the related research literature, I came across the theory of *cultural shock and adaptation* (Winkelman, 1994). This anthropological theory posits that when individuals enter a new cultural setting that is significantly different from their own, they go through cyclical stages of *tourist*, *crisis*, *adjustment*, and *adaptation* in order to function in the site and among its populace. I made the connection that the teacher I was observing had gone through (and was still going through) these stages as she adjusted her practice to better instruct the children from a cultural background different from hers. The theory of cultural shock and adaptation was not applied at the very beginning of the study, but later on as fieldwork progressed and the central observational focus evolved. This theoretical glue now held everything together. My study was not an attempt to support or disprove the cultural shock and adaptation theory. The established theory was there to *guide* and *advise* me as I traveled on my own qualitative journey. Any new and original theories that could be developed from fieldwork were my responsibility.

As for the methodological premises of a conceptual framework, these refer to the reasons for your choices of data collection and analytic methods. If your researcher's lens sees representations of what it means to be human in its most elegant, distilled, and essential terms, then your methodological premises are phenomenological. If your researcher's lens sees images of symbolic and metaphoric representations of the human condition through the strategic use of line, color, texture, and other visual elements, then your methodological premises are arts based. Methodological premises relate closely to the genres of qualitative research and their associated methods, and the conceptual framework narrative now asks that you *rationalize why* you are choosing one particular genre and its associated methods over the others. Refer back to Chapter 2 for the data analytic advantages of such methods as interviews and participant observation.

But there are also more interpretive genres of qualitative research, such as narrative and poetic inquiry, which do not overtly state in their publications what epistemological, theoretical, or methodological premises are driving the work. In fact, to do so would diminish the power and aesthetic effect of the representation by mixing incompatible elements. I once reviewed a journal article submission of a powerful autoethnographic poem whose flow and mood were interrupted with unnecessary footnotes of biographical background information. I advised the author, "If you feel the need to footnote your creative work, then the poetry's not doing its job." Most all of the world's great literary masterpieces are not prefaced with explanatory paragraphs by their authors on why they wrote the work or what guidelines were followed in their development. The work stands alone and speaks for itself through the reader's interpretation of it.

Like all other aspects of qualitative research, the conceptual framework can evolve as the study proceeds and can even change midway through a study. For purposes of research design, the conceptual framework consists of a brief discussion of the epistemological, theoretical, and methodological premises that frame your study. These are sometimes discussed in a proposal's or finished product's review of the related research literature. At other times they are discussed at the very beginning of the work to frame the reader for the study's and researcher's position. And yet at other times the conceptual framework is discussed as a separate section just before the description of the "Method" (e.g., a profile of the participants and the site, duration of the fieldwork, data collection and analytic procedures, etc.) in more traditional academic write-ups.

Is a conceptual framework always necessary for a qualitative research project? There are actually two answers to this question: (1) no, but it certainly helps; and (2) it depends on which research genre you select. Virtually every methodologist asserts that all studies are driven by theory, whether the researcher is aware of it or not. Sometimes it helps to know that there is most likely a label, term, or construct for the way you're thinking as your research design comes together. Reading a variety of published qualitative reports about your topic gives you an idea of how some writers have integrated previously developed theories into their studies.

IRB Application and Review

The research design is not just an opportunity to outline the preliminary details and processes of your project before you begin; it is also necessary preparatory work for written application to an Institutional Review Board (IRB, as it is known in the United States). Depending on your organizational or institutional affiliation, the proposed site and participants for your study, and the research topic itself, you may be required to first get official approval by an oversight committee charged to review proposed studies with "human subjects." The purpose of an IRB is to insure that its institutional representatives are conducting research with humans in an ethical manner and in compliance with governmental and legal regulations. Such oversight boards were originally formed to monitor the conduct of experimental and biomedical research, but they now include education and the social and behavioral sciences, and their naturalistic studies and field experiments in qualitative inquiry.

The specific application processes and forms vary from site to site, but you will be required to submit such details as: a narrative description of the research study, the estimated duration of the project, the number and ages of participants you plan to study, how the data will be collected and stored, what steps you'll be taking to insure participant confidentiality and anonymity (for example, using pseudonyms for participants instead of their actual names), the potential risks to those involved with your research, and how the results of the study will be disseminated. Attachments may also be required that address such matters as: the types of interview questions you plan to ask, consent forms you will distribute to participants for their review and signature, and any sample instruments such as written surveys or questionnaires. If necessary, the IRB may ask the applicant to be present during committee review of the proposal in case members need to ask questions, get more information about the project, or raise issues of concern. Depending on the fieldwork site, such as a public school, you may also need its administrators' review and permission to conduct the study there, especially if it involves children or other vulnerable populations. Research with children in nonschool settings will almost always require parental/guardian consent.

All researchers must exhibit ethical conduct with participants, but there has been much recent debate surrounding the utility of IRBs and their restrictive expectations as they relate to naturalistic, qualitative inquiry. The paradigm is an emergent model, yet IRB applications, for example, will require that the researcher list the specific numbers and ages of participants to be involved and require that all planned interview questions be submitted beforehand. Committee review members unfamiliar with the evolutionary processes of qualitative research are unsympathetic to "to be determined" answers on an application form. Nevertheless, the process is mandatory if the institution for which you work or where you study requires such compliance. List what is projected and most likely to occur at the beginning of the research project on the IRB application and update the committee with more specifics about your approved study as fieldwork proceeds. Also, check your discipline's professional associations and societies for guidelines for the ethical conduct of research with human participants.

An IRB application form, despite its minor flaws, actually serves as an excellent template for a qualitative research design. The information that must be entered forces you to think through most of the methodological and logistical matters involved with a study. And its submission as one application packet brings everything together for committee review and, hopefully, constructive feedback for research design revision.

Closure

Qualitative research design is a carefully thought through narrative of preliminary decisions that harmonize and provide initial guidance for the investigator's fieldwork. Early concurrent matters involve selecting the specific topic, reviewing the related research literature, composing the project's statement of purpose, and drafting a central question and related research ones. Conceptual framework matters, which include the epistemological, theoretical, and methodological premises that drive the study, are also considered during the early stages of the proposal, and as a through line throughout the remaining research design decisions and the study itself. Appropriate participants and field sites are selected, along with the data collection and data analytic methods that will best address the research purpose and questions. The study's final representational and presentational forms are considered, along with reflection on possible intrinsic outcomes for all involved with the project. Finally, application, review, and approval of the study by an IRB panel or other overseeing body (such as a thesis or dissertation committee) better assures initial ethical and legal compliance by the researcher.

Qualitative data analysis and writing matters are addressed next.

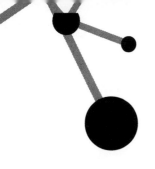

4

A SURVEY OF
QUALITATIVE DATA
ANALYTIC METHODS

DATA ANALYSIS is often given short shrift in introductory textbooks on qualitative research. Therefore, I devote a major portion of this book to the topic to provide readers with a more comprehensive overview. But it is still an incomplete portrait of the process, for qualitative data analysis can be intricate and, at times, conceptual and abstract. Nevertheless, I focus on what I perceive as analytic fundamentals with a few examples to illustrate selected methods.

One approach to understanding the social world is to discern its patterns and to construct human meanings that seem to capture life's essences and essentials. Thus, the purpose and outcome of data analysis is to reveal to others through fresh insights what we've observed and discovered about the human condition. Just as there are a variety of genres, elements, and styles of qualitative research, so too are there a variety of methods available for qualitative data analysis. Analytic choices are most often based on what methods will harmonize with your genre selection and conceptual framework, what will generate the most sufficient answers to your research questions, and what will best represent and present the project's findings.

Analysis can range from the factual to the conceptual to the interpretive. Analysis can also range from a straightforward descriptive account to an emergently constructed grounded theory to an evocatively composed short story. A qualitative research project's outcomes may range from rigorously achieved, insightful answers, to open-ended, evocative questions; from rich descriptive detail to a bullet-pointed list of themes; and from third-person, objective reportage to first-person, emotion-laden poetry. Just as there are multiple destinations in qualitative research, there are multiple pathways and journeys along the way.

Since qualitative research's design, fieldwork, and data collection are most often provisional, emergent, and evolutionary processes, you reflect on and analyze the data *as* you gather them and proceed through the project. If preplanned methods are not working, you change them to secure the data you need. There is generally a postfieldwork period when continued reflection and more systematic data analysis occur, concurrent with or followed by additional data collection, if needed, and the more formal write-up of the study, which is in itself an analytic act. Through fieldnote writing, interview transcribing, analytic memo writing, and other documentation processes, you gain cognitive ownership of your data, and the intuitive, tacit, synthesizing capabilities of your brain begin sensing patterns, making connections, and seeing the bigger picture. But there are also systematic ways of reorganizing and reflecting on your qualitative data to help you along.

Methodologist Robert E. Stake (1995) observes, "Good research is not so much about good methods as much as it is about good thinking" (p. 19). Thus, a brief discussion of how to "think qualitatively" is addressed first.

Pattern Construction

The natural world is filled with patterns because we, as humans, have constructed them as such. Stars in the night sky are not just a random assembly; our ancestors pieced them together to form constellations like the Big Dipper. A collection of flowers growing wild in a field has a pattern, as does an individual flower's patterns of leaves and petals. Look at the physical objects humans have created and notice how pattern oriented we are in our construction, organization, and decoration. Look around you in your environment and notice how many patterns are evident on your clothing, in a room, and on most objects themselves. Even our daily and long-term human actions are reproduced patterns in the form of roles, rules, routines, and rituals.

This human propensity for pattern making follows us into qualitative data analysis. From the vast array of interview transcripts, fieldnotes, documents, and other forms of data, there is this instinctive, hardwired need to bring order to the collection—to not just reorganize it, but to look for and construct patterns out of it. The discernment of patterns is one of the first steps in the data analytic process, and the methods described later are recommended ways to do so.

Category Construction

Humans also categorize things in innumerable ways. Think of an average apartment or house's layout. Why is the toilet not next to the refrigerator? Why is a working television not in a closet? The rooms of a dwelling have been constructed or categorized by their builders and occupants according to function. A kitchen is designated as an area to store and prepare food and the cooking and dining materials such as pots, pans, utensils, and so on. A bedroom is designated for sleeping, a closet for clothing storage, a bathroom for bodily functions and hygiene, and so on. Each room is like a *category* in which related and relevant *patterns of human action* occur. Of course, there are exceptions now and then, such as eating breakfast in bed rather than in a dining area, or living in a small studio apartment in which most possessions are contained within one large room (but nonetheless are most often organized and clustered into subcategories according to function and optimal use of space).

The point here is that the patterns of social action we designate into particular categories during qualitative data analysis are not perfectly bounded. Category construction is our best attempt to cluster the most seemingly alike things into the most seemingly appropriate groups. Categorizing is organizing and ordering the vast array of data from a study because it is from these larger and meaning-rich units that we can better grasp the particular features of each one, and the categories' possible interrelationships with one another.

Interaction, Interplay, and Interrelationship

Another task of qualitative data analysis is to explore the ways our patterns and categories *interact* and *interplay*. I use these terms to suggest the qualitative equivalent of statistical correlation, but interaction and interplay are much more than a simple relationship—they imply *interrelationship*. Interaction refers to reverberative connections—for example, how one or more categories might influence and affect the others, how categories operate concurrently, or whether there is some kind of "domino" effect to them. Interplay refers to the structural and processual nature of categories—for example, whether some type of sequential order, hierarchy, or taxonomy exists, whether any overlaps occur, whether there is superordinate and subordinate arrangement, and what types of organizational frameworks or networks might exist among them. There can even be patterns of patterns and categories of categories if your mind thinks conceptually and abstractly enough.

Recall my earlier discussion that the positivist construct "cause and effect" becomes *influences and affects* in qualitative analysis. Our minds can intricately connect multiple phenomena together, but only if the data and their analyses support the constructions. If I asked you to list some factors that lead to university-level student success, you might propose such things as: a strong work ethic, a sense of belonging, supportive faculty, relevant coursework, peer communities, intrinsic motivation, financial resources, and others. But if I asked you to speculate on how these categories might interact and interplay, interesting webs of connection may emerge. For example, you may propose that a sense of belonging is cultivated when supportive faculty *and* peer communities are present. Supportive faculty may intrinsically motivate some students to cultivate a strong work ethic, peer communities may appear competitive and thus encourage the development of a strong work ethic, or some students may step foot on campus with a strong work ethic and intrinsic motivation already embedded within them. Perhaps supportive faculty *and* peer communities *and* intrinsic motivation make your work ethic even stronger. And perhaps relevant coursework from supportive faculty enhances intrinsic motivation, which develops a strong work ethic.... And so on and so on and so on. We can speculate about the interaction and inter-play all we want, but it is only through a more systematic investiga-tion of the data—in other words, good thinking—that we can plausibly establish any possible interrelationships.

Deductive, Inductive, and Abductive Reasoning

Unlike quantitative research, with its statistical formulas and estab-lished hypothesis-testing protocols, qualitative research has no standardized methods of data analysis. Rest assured, there are rec-ommended guidelines from the field's scholars and a legacy of ana-lytic strategies from which to draw. But the primary heuristics (or, methods of discovery) you apply during a study are *deductive*, *inductive*, and *abductive* reasoning.

Deduction is what we generally draw and conclude from estab-lished facts and evidence. Induction is what we explore and infer to be transferable from the particular to the general, based on an examination of the evidence and an accumulation of knowledge. Abduction is surmising from the evidence that which is most likely, those explanatory hunches based on clues. "Whereas deduc-tive inferences are certain (so long as their premises are true) and inductive inferences are probable, abductive inferences are merely plausible" (Shank, 2008, p. 1).

For example, in my very first ethnographic fieldwork project, I observed a class of junior high school–level students in an inner-city neighborhood over the course of several months. I did not begin my observations with any particular agenda those first few weeks; I simply observed teenage social life as it unfolded before me to get a general feel for the group's subculture. This was observ-ing and working *inductively*, for I was looking at the "evidence" of student actions and talk across time and accumulating knowledge about this specific site.

On one particular school day, I saw a young man enter the class-room wearing a brown T-shirt and black jeans. There was certainly nothing unusual about that, until I observed a young woman entering the classroom also wearing a brown T-shirt and black jeans. And then another young man came in wearing the exact same colored clothing. Here was a pattern that caught my attention, and I began to think *abductively* for a reason why three adolescents in the same classroom on the same day were wearing similarly colored clothes. Abduction explores the most plausible explanation from an array of possibilities, but the immediate association that came to mind was a memory of my own high school "uniform": all marching band members wore red shirts and white pants on pep rally days, so I assumed this clothing pattern was something comparable at this school since it generally happened on Fridays. It could also have been mere coincidence that the three students wore comparable outfits on a single day, but the odds of the same three people all wearing brown T-shirts and black jeans on several successive Fridays meant that the action had to have been purposeful.

But my thinking was flawed, for I jumped to a conclusion—a *deduction*—too early without considering other possibilities or investigating all the facts. I was slightly embarrassed at my misassumptions and cultural naiveté when I later interviewed some teachers at the school and learned that selected students who wore brown T-shirts and black jeans on Fridays were members of a local neighborhood gang proudly displaying their colors and affiliation. I learned from this new knowledge that my inductive and abductive thinking processes needed to slow down, to broaden my worldview and learn the subtleties of the school culture I was observing, and to humbly ask others questions about things that puzzled or surprised me, rather than assume I could automatically deduce all the answers I needed.

It is not always necessary to know the names of these three ways of thinking as you're proceeding through analysis. In fact, you will more than likely reverberate quickly from one to another depending on the task at hand. But what's important to remember about thinking is: don't take the obvious for granted; sometimes the expected won't always happen; your hunches can be quite right and, at other times, quite wrong; examine the evidence carefully and make reasonable inferences; and logically yet imaginatively think about what's going on and how it all comes together. Futurists and inventors propose three questions when they think about creating new visions for the world: What is possible (induction)? What is plausible (abduction)? What is preferable (deduction)?

These same three questions might be posed as you proceed through qualitative data analysis.

Data Intimacy

Analysis is accelerated as you take cognitive ownership of your data. By reading and rereading the corpus, you gain intimate familiarity with its contents and begin to notice significant details as well as make new insights about their meanings. Patterns, categories, and their interrelationships become more evident the more you know the subtleties of the database.

Qualitative data analysis is concurrent with data collection and management. As interviews are transcribed, fieldnotes fleshed out, and documents filed, the researcher uses the opportunity to read the corpus and make preliminary notations directly on the data documents by highlighting, bolding, italicizing, or noting in some way the salient portions. As these data are initially reviewed, the researcher also composes supplemental analytic memos (discussed later) that include first impressions, reminders for follow-up, preliminary connections, and other thinking matters about the phenomena at work.

Now that these very basic ways of thinking qualitatively have been reviewed, the discussion turns to a selected number of ways to analyze qualitative data. The following is a broad repertoire of methods from which to choose for your particular study, but which one(s) you use depends on which genre of qualitative research has been selected.

Codes and Coding—Process Coding

Coding is a heuristic—a method of discovery—to the meanings of individual sections of data. These codes function as a way of patterning, classifying, and later reorganizing each datum into emergent categories for further analysis. Different types of codes exist for different types of genres and analytic approaches, but this chapter will focus on only a few methods.

> A code in qualitative data analysis is most often a word or short phrase that symbolically assigns a summative, salient, essence-capturing, and/or evocative attribute for a portion of

language-based or visual data. The data can consist of interview transcripts, participant observation fieldnotes, journals, documents, literature, artifacts, photographs, video, websites, e-mail correspondence, and so on. The portion of data to be coded can… range in magnitude from a single word to a full sentence to an entire page of text to a stream of moving images…. Just as a title represents and captures a book or film or poem's primary content and essence, so does a code represent and capture a datum's primary content and essence. (Saldaña, 2009, p. 3)

As a first example, the following interview excerpt about a young woman's career development is coded in the right-hand margin in capital letters. The superscript numbers match the datum unit with its code. The method is called process coding, which uses gerunds ("-ing" words) exclusively to capture action in the data (Charmaz, 2002; Corbin & Strauss, 2008). Notice that the interviewer's portions are not coded, just the participants'. A code is applied each time the subtopic of the interview shifts, and the same codes can (and should) be used more than once if the subtopics are similar:

I (Interviewer): Where do you see yourself five years from now in your career?

P (Participant): [1] Well, I hope to be teaching at a university somewhere on the East Coast. [2] But times being what they are, I don't know if that's possible.

[1] HOPING

[2] DOUBTING

I: You mean the economy?

P: Yeah. I may have to stay at my current job, assuming that I don't get pink slipped. [3] But hey, at least I've got a job, that's something.

[3] BEING GRATEFUL

I: Are you actively looking for another job now?

P: [4] I've picked up the Job Search newsletter and looked through it just to see what's out there, [5] but I think it's too early to leave here. I've gotta get some more years under my belt before I start applying—you know,

[4] JOB SEARCHING

[5] GAINING EXPERIENCE

more experience to make me look like I know my stuff. [6] But, I also check some online job search sites each day, check my e-mails to see if there's any response to letters I've sent out. [7] Friends tell me to just keep looking, something eventually turns up, so I hope they're right.

[6] JOB SEARCHING

[7] HOPING

Different researchers analyzing this same piece of data may develop completely different codes, depending on their lenses and filters. The above codes are only one person's interpretation of what is happening in the data, not the definitive list. The process codes have transformed the raw data units into new representations for analysis. A listing of them applied to this interview transcript, in the order they appear, reads:

HOPING
DOUBTING
BEING GRATEFUL
JOB SEARCHING
GAINING EXPERIENCE
JOB SEARCHING
HOPING

The codes are then classified into similar clusters. Obviously, the same codes share the same category, but it is also possible that a single code can stand on its own if you feel it is unique enough. Notice that once the codes have been classified, a category label is applied to them. Like the process codes, the category names are also in the form of gerunds to connote action:

Category 1: Career Building

CODE: JOB SEARCHING
CODE: JOB SEARCHING
CODE: GAINING EXPERIENCE

Category 2: Feeling In-Between

CODE: HOPING
CODE: HOPING
CODE: DOUBTING
CODE: BEING GRATEFUL

The two categories, **Career Building** and **Feeling In-Between**, are then reflected upon for how they might interact and interplay. This is where the next major facet of data analysis, analytic memos, enters the scheme.

Analytic Memos—"Think Pieces"

Like fieldnote writing, perspectives vary among practitioners as to the methods for documenting the researcher's analytic insights and subjective experiences. Some advise that such reflections should be included in fieldnote OCs as relevant to the data. Others advise that a separate researcher's journal should be maintained for recording these impressions. And still others advise that these thoughts be documented as separate analytic memos. I prescribe the latter as a method because it is generated by and directly connected to the data themselves.

An analytic memo is a "think piece" of reflexive freewriting, a narrative that sets in words your interpretations of the data. Coding and categorizing are heuristics to detect some of the possible patterns at work within the corpus, and an analytic memo further articulates your deductive, inductive, and abductive thinking processes on what things may mean. What follows is an example of an analytic memo based on the coded and categorized interview transcript above. It is not intended as the final write-up for a publication, but as an open-ended reflection on the phenomena and processes suggested by the data and their analysis thus far. As the study proceeds, however, initial and substantive analytic memos can be revisited and revised for eventual integration into the report itself.

Note how the memo is given a title for future and further categorization, how participant quotes are occasionally included for evidentiary support, and how the category names are bolded and the codes kept in capital letters to show how they integrate or weave into the thinking:

July 29, 2009

EMERGENT CATEGORIES: THE EMOTIONS OF
CAREER BUILDING

A **Career Building** trajectory is not just a matter of education and skills, it's a matter of emotional resilience. The current economic downturn has placed the participant literally and emotionally IN-BETWEEN current and future employment prospects. The participant's feelings ebb and flow in this narrative, suggesting a lack of stability and security, even though she states, "at least I've got a job, that's something." It seems like the emotions of JOB SEARCHING also have a trajectory continuum, from its negative DOUBT, to its middle-ground gratitude (BEING GRATEFUL), to its optimistic and future-oriented HOPING for opportunity. There's a self-defeating tone throughout this interview excerpt. The participant takes positive actions to advance her career, but then quickly negates the efforts with DOUBT.

JOB SEARCHING is HOPING. Early **Career Building** in this case is perhaps not so much a smooth trajectory of one job successively followed by a better one, but more a period of experience-building stasis in which **Feeling In-Between** overlaps with current and future prospects.

Though the metaphor is a bit flawed and limiting, think of codes and their consequent categories as separate picture puzzle pieces, and their integration into an analytic memo as the assembly of the picture.

Codes and Coding—In Vivo Coding

The first example of coding illustrated process coding. A second frequently applied method is called in vivo coding. The root meaning of "in vivo" is "in that which is alive" and refers to a code based on the actual language used by the participant (Strauss, 1987). What words or phrases you select as codes are those that seem to stand out as significant or summative of what's being said. I recommend that in vivo codes be placed in quotation marks as a way of designating that the code is extracted directly from the data record. Using the same transcript of the job-searching participant, in vivo codes are listed in the right-hand column. Note that instead of seven codes used for process coding, the total number of in vivo codes is eleven. This is not to suggest that there should be specific numbers or ranges of codes used for particular methods. In vivo codes, though, tend to be applied more frequently to data. Again, the interviewer's questions and prompts are not coded, just the participant's responses:

I (Interviewer): Where do you see yourself five years from now in your career?	
P (Participant): Well, [1] I hope to be teaching at a university somewhere on the East Coast. But [2] times being what they are, I don't know if that's possible.	[1] "I HOPE" [2] "TIMES BEING WHAT THEY ARE"
I: You mean the economy?	
P: Yeah. I may have to stay at my current job, assuming that I don't get [3] pink slipped. But hey, [4] at least I've got a job, that's something.	[3] "PINK SLIPPED" [4] "AT LEAST I'VE GOT A JOB"
I: Are you actively looking for another job now?	
P: I've picked up the Job Search newsletter and looked through it just to see what's out there, but I think it's [5] too early to leave here.	[5] "TOO EARLY"
I've gotta get some [6] more years under my belt before I start applying— you know, more experience to make me look like [7] I know my stuff. But, I also [8] check some online job search sites each day, [9] check my e-mails to see if there's any response to letters I've sent out. Friends tell me to just [10] keep looking, something eventually turns up, so [11] I hope they're right.	[6] "MORE YEARS UNDER MY BELT" [7] "I KNOW MY STUFF" [8] "CHECK" [9] "CHECK" [10] "KEEP LOOKING" [11] "I HOPE"

The in vivo codes are then extracted from the transcript and listed in the order they appear to prepare them for analytic reflection:

"I HOPE"
"TIMES BEING WHAT THEY ARE"
"PINK SLIPPED"
"AT LEAST I'VE GOT A JOB"

"TOO EARLY"
"MORE YEARS UNDER MY BELT"
"I KNOW MY STUFF"
"CHECK"
"CHECK"
"KEEP LOOKING"
"I HOPE"

Like process coding, the in vivo codes are now clustered into similar categories, but notice how the grouping is different this time due to the nature of the codes. Also, the categorizing is based on the researcher's interpretation—a different researcher may have grouped these eleven codes in a completely different way. And, there is no particular reason why there are only two categories—the number could have expanded to three, perhaps even four, depending on the analyst's thinking processes:

Category 1: Optimistic Outlook

IN VIVO CODES:

"I HOPE"
"AT LEAST I'VE GOT A JOB"
"I KNOW MY STUFF"
"CHECK"
"CHECK"
"KEEP LOOKING"
"I HOPE"

Category 2: Pessimistic Outlook

IN VIVO CODES:

"TIMES BEING WHAT THEY ARE"
"PINK SLIPPED"
"TOO EARLY"
"MORE YEARS UNDER MY BELT"

The word choices of OPTIMISTIC and PESSIMISTIC emerged as *dimensions* in these codes. Though not always necessary for analysis, one component is to examine what *ranges* or *variability* exist in the data, and what struck the researcher in this set of codes are the varying dimensions of the *property* of one's career OUTLOOK.

Now that the codes have been clustered into two tentative categories, an analytic memo is composed to expand on the rationale.

Analytic Memos–Topics for Reflection

There are several recommended topic areas for analytic memo writing throughout the qualitative study. Memos are opportunities to reflect on and write about:

- how you personally relate to the participants and/or the phenomenon
- your study's research questions
- your code choices and their operational definitions
- the emergent patterns, categories, themes, and concepts
- the possible networks (links, connections, overlaps, flows) among the codes, patterns, categories, themes, and concepts
- an emergent or related existent theory
- any problems with the study
- any personal or ethical dilemmas with the study
- future directions for the study
- the analytic memos generated thus far [labeled "metamemos"]
- the final report for the study (Saldaña, 2009, p. 40)

Since writing *is* analysis, analytic memos expand on the inferential meanings of the truncated codes and categories as a transitional stage into a more coherent narrative. A few analytic memos related to the in vivo–coded data above now follow. Notice that the memo titles are composed of the type of memo, followed by a unique subtitle that captures the content or major idea of the narrative:

August 14, 2009

RELATING TO THE PARTICIPANTS AND/OR THE
PHENOMENON: MY EARLY
JOB SEARCHES

I too remember how optimistic I felt as a senior at the university, sure to land a job as soon as I graduated. I did do several interviews, but the results were not in my favor. I felt so confident in what I knew, so why wasn't I being hired? It wasn't until later that I realized those errors I made—not fully answering the interviewer's questions; saying what I thought was a funny remark, only to be taken the wrong way; or feeling that I could request for things to be done my way and not the organization's way.

Optimism (confidence?) should not be confused with cockiness. The latter will come back to haunt you and bite you every time.

August 15, 2009

EMERGENT CATEGORIES: AN OPTIMISTIC AND PESSIMISTIC OUTLOOK

A *property* of a career trajectory is one's **Outlook**; the *dimensions* of an outlook range from **Optimistic** to **Pessimistic**.

The old saying goes, "Is the glass half empty or half full?" **Outlook** influences and affects a career trajectory. Even when someone's locked in a less than desirable situation, career building can be **Optimistic** when one takes constructive action to job search. **Pessimism** emerges when doubt about one's abilities or career prospects, or economic circumstances beyond one's control, enters the equation. One can vacillate rapidly between an **Optimistic** and **Pessimistic Outlook** or career perception and its realization.

Playing with the word, one "outlooks" and one "looks out" for one's career. **Outlook** is both a perception and an action; and the perception shapes the actions. A career is "HOPE"fully waiting for doors to open, but it's also taking the initiative to go up to the doors and knock ("KEEP LOOKING," "CHECK," "CHECK").

Like categorized codes, analytic memos are eventually clustered by similarity of topic, then revised and edited to eventually become substantive portions of the final report.

Codes and Coding—Additional Methods

The examples thus far have demonstrated only two specific coding methods of at least thirty documented approaches (Saldaña, 2009). Which one(s) you choose for your analysis depends on such factors as your conceptual framework, the genre of qualitative research for your project, the types of data you collect, and so on. Just a few of the other approaches available for coding qualitative data that you may find useful as starting points are:

Descriptive Coding

Descriptive codes (Miles & Huberman, 1994) are primarily nouns that simply summarize the topic of a datum. This coding approach is particularly useful when you have different types of data gathered for one study, such as interview transcripts, fieldnotes, and documents. Descriptive codes not only help categorize but also index the data corpus' basic contents for further analytic work. An example of a fieldnote coded descriptively follows; note that a few of them double as in vivo codes as well:

I: Are you actively looking for another job now?
P: [1] I've picked up the Job Search   [1] "JOB SEARCH"
newsletter and looked through it just to
see what's out there, [2] but I think it's too   [2] "EXPERIENCE"
early to leave here. I've gotta get some
more years under my belt before I start
applying—you know, more experience
to make me look like I know my stuff.
[3] But, I also check some online job search   [3] "JOB SEARCH"
sites each day, [4] check my e-mails to see   [4] FOLLOW-UP
if there's any response to letters I've sent
out. [5] Friends tell me to just keep looking, [5] ENCOURAGEMENT
something eventually turns up, so I hope
they're right.

For initial analysis, descriptive codes are clustered into similar categories to detect such patterns as frequency (i.e., categories with the largest number of codes), interrelationship (i.e., categories that seem to connect in some way), and initial work for grounded theory development (discussed later).

Values Coding

Values coding (LeCompte & Preissle, 1993; Saldaña, 2009) identifies the values, attitudes, and beliefs of a participant, as shared by
the individual and/or interpreted by the analyst. This coding
method infers the "heart and mind" of an individual or group's
worldview as to what is important, perceived as true, maintained
as opinion, and felt strongly. The three constructs are part of a
complex interconnected system. Briefly, a value (V) is what we
attribute as important, be it a person, thing, or idea. An attitude
(A) is the evaluative way we think and feel about ourselves, others,
things, or ideas. A belief (B) is what we think and feel as true or
necessary, formed from our "personal knowledge, experiences,
opinions, prejudices, morals, and other interpretive perceptions of
the social world" (Saldaña, 2009, pp. 89–90). Values coding
explores intrapersonal, interpersonal, and cultural constructs or
ethos. It is an admittedly slippery task to code this way, for it is
sometimes difficult to discern what is a value, attitude, or belief
because they are intricately interrelated. But the depth you can
potentially obtain is rich. An example of values coding follows:

P: Well, [1] I hope to be teaching at a   [1] V: UNIVERSITY
university somewhere on the East Coast.   PROFESSORIATE
But [2] times being what they are, I don't   [2] B: CAREER
know if that's possible.   LIMITATIONS
I: You mean the economy?
P: Yeah. I may have to stay at my current
job, assuming that I don't get pink
slipped. [3] But hey, at least I've got a job,   [3] A: GRATITUDE
that's something.

For analysis, categorize the codes for each of the three different
constructs together (i.e., all values in one group, attitudes in a
second group, and beliefs in a third group). Analytic memo writing about the patterns and possible interrelationships may reveal a
more detailed and intricate worldview of the participant.

Dramaturgical Coding

Dramaturgical coding (Berg, 2001; Feldman, 1995; Goffman, 1959;
Saldaña, 2005) perceives life as performance and its participants
as characters in a social drama. Codes are assigned to the data

(i.e., a "play script") that analyze the characters in action, reaction, and interaction. Dramaturgical coding of participants examines their *objectives* (OBJ) or wants, needs, and motives; the *conflicts* (CON) or obstacles they face as they try to achieve their objectives; the *tactics* (TAC) or strategies they employ to reach their objectives; their *attitudes* (ATT) toward others and their given circumstances; the particular *emotions* (EMO) they experience throughout; and their *subtexts* (SUB) or underlying and unspoken thoughts. In the coding example thus far, we know that this participant's OBJ [objective] is a UNIVERSITY TEACHING POSITION, but her ATT [attitude] toward getting one is PESSIMISTIC. We can infer her EMO [emotions], just as audience members do when we see a character on stage or in film. Perhaps this job-seeking individual, based on the text alone, may feel INSECURE. But the researcher actually present at the interview, seeing her open body language and hearing her upbeat vocal tones, may have inferred that her emotions were actually CONFIDENT and HOPEFUL:

I: Are you actively looking for another job now?
P: [1] I've picked up the Job Search newsletter and looked through it just to see what's out there, but [2] I think it's too early to leave here. I've gotta get some more years under my belt before I start applying—you know, more experience to make me look like I know my stuff. [3] But, I also check some online job search sites each day, check my e-mails to see if there's any response to letters I've sent out. [4] Friends tell me to just keep looking, something eventually turns up, so I hope they're right.

[1] TAC: READING JOB NEWSLETTER
[2] CON: INSUFFICIENT EXPERIENCE

[3] TAC: ONLINE FOLLOW-UP

[4] SUB: RESILIENCE

For analysis, group similar codes together (e.g., all objectives in one group, all conflicts in another group, all tactics in a third group, etc.). Explore how the individuals or groups manage problem solving in their daily lives. Dramaturgical coding is particularly useful as preliminary work for narrative inquiry story development or performance-based research representations such as ethnodrama.

Versus Coding

Versus coding (Hager, Maier, O'Hara, Ott, & Saldaña, 2000; Wolcott, 2003) identifies the conflicts, struggles, and power issues observed in social action, reaction, and interaction as an X VS. Y code, such as: MEN VS. WOMEN, CONSERVATIVES VS. LIBERALS, FAITH VS. LOGIC, and so on. Conflicts are rarely this dichotomous—they are typically nuanced and much more complex. But humans tend to perceive these struggles with an US VS. THEM mindset. The codes can range from the observable to the conceptual and can be applied to data that show humans in tension with others, themselves, or ideologies:

P: [1] Well, I hope to be teaching at a university somewhere on the East Coast. But times being what they are, I don't know if that's possible.
I: You mean the economy?

[1] CAREER DREAMS VS. BAD ECONOMY

P: Yeah. [2] I may have to stay at my current job, assuming that I don't get pink slipped. But hey, at least I've got a job, that's something.
I: Are you actively looking for another job now?

[2] JOB SECURITY VS. BAD ECONOMY

P: [3] I've picked up the Job Search newsletter and looked through it just to see what's out there, but I think it's too early to leave here. I've gotta get some more years under my belt before I start applying—you know, more experience to make me look like I know my stuff.

[3] ADVANCEMENT VS. "MORE EXPERIENCE"

As an initial analytic tactic, group the versus codes into one of three categories: the *Stakeholders*, their *Perceptions and/or Actions*, and the *Issues* at stake. Examine how the three interrelate and identify the central ideological conflict at work as an **X vs. Y** category. Analytic memos and the narrative can detail the nuances of the issues.

Remember that what has been profiled above is a broad brushstroke description of just a few basic coding processes, several of which can be compatibly "mixed and matched" within a single analysis.

Certainly with additional data, more in-depth analysis can occur, but coding is only one approach to extracting and constructing preliminary meaning from the data corpus. What now follows are additional methods for qualitative analysis.

Themeing the Data

Unlike codes, which are most often single words or short phrases that symbolically represent a datum, themes are extended phrases or sentences that summarize the manifest (apparent) and latent (underlying) meanings of data (Auerbach & Silverstein, 2003; Boyatzis, 1998). Themes, too, can be categorized, or listed in superordinate and subordinate outline formats as an analytic tactic. Below is the interview transcript example used in the coding sections above. (Hopefully you're not too fatigued at this point with the transcript, but it's important to know how inquiry with the same data set can be approached in several different ways.) Notice how themeing interprets what is happening through the use of two distinct phrases—A CAREER IS (i.e., manifest or apparent meanings) and A CAREER MEANS (i.e., latent or underlying meanings):

I: Where do you see yourself five years from now in your career?
P: [1] Well, I hope to be teaching at a university somewhere on the East Coast. [2] But times being what they are, I don't know if that's possible.
I: You mean the economy?
P: Yeah. I may have to stay at my current job, assuming that I don't get pink slipped. But hey, at least I've got a job, that's something.
I: Are you actively looking for another job now?
P: [3] I've picked up the Job Search newsletter and looked through it just to see what's out there, but [4] I think it's too early to leave here. I've gotta get some more years under my belt before I start applying—you know, more experience to make me look like I know my stuff. [5] But, I also check some online job search sites each day,

[1] A CAREER IS GEOGRAPHIC
[2] A CAREER IS DETERMINED BY ECONOMIC FORCES

[3] A CAREER IS INQUIRY
[4] A CAREER MEANS CULTIVATING EXPERTISE

[5] A CAREER IS DAILY MAINTENANCE

check my e-mails to see if there's
any response to letters I've sent out.
[6] Friends tell me to just keep looking,   [6] A CAREER MEANS
something eventually turns up, so I   PERSEVERANCE
hope they're right.

Unlike the seven process codes and eleven in vivo codes in the examples above, there are now six themes to work with. In the order they appear, they are:

A CAREER IS GEOGRAPHIC
A CAREER IS DETERMINED BY ECONOMIC FORCES
A CAREER IS INQUIRY
A CAREER MEANS CULTIVATING EXPERTISE
A CAREER IS DAILY MAINTENANCE
A CAREER MEANS PERSEVERANCE

There are several ways to categorize the themes as preparation for analytic memo writing. The first is to arrange them in outline format with superordinate and subordinate levels, based on how the themes seem to take organizational shape and structure. Simply "cutting and pasting" the themes in multiple arrangements on a word processor page eventually develops a sense of order to them. For example:

I.   A CAREER IS DETERMINED BY ECONOMIC FORCES
II. A CAREER IS GEOGRAPHIC
III. A CAREER MEANS PERSEVERANCE
    A. A CAREER IS INQUIRY
    B. A CAREER IS DAILY MAINTENANCE
    C. A CAREER MEANS CULTIVATING EXPERTISE

A second approach is to categorize the themes into similar clusters and to develop different category labels or *theoretical constructs*. A theoretical construct is an abstraction that transforms the central phenomenon's themes into broader applications but can still use "is" and "means" as prompts to capture the bigger picture at work. Notice that one of the construct labels below adapts a keyword from one of its themes since the idea seems to best summarize what the themes have in common:

Theoretical Construct 1: A Career Is Time and Place

Supporting Themes:

A CAREER IS DETERMINED BY ECONOMIC FORCES
A CAREER IS GEOGRAPHIC

Theoretical Construct 2: A Career Is Perseverance

Supporting Themes:
A CAREER MEANS PERSEVERANCE
A CAREER IS INQUIRY
A CAREER IS DAILY MAINTENANCE
A CAREER MEANS CULTIVATING EXPERTISE

What follows next is an analytic memo generated from the "cut and paste" arrangement of themes into theoretical constructs:

August 2, 2009

EMERGENT THEMES: CAREER AND TIME

A career is not a thing, it's a process. A career is **time** and **place**. A career is **time** to get to **place**, driven by one's **perseverance**. Careers are not guaranteed; one "works" for work, and that takes **time**.

Time seems to be a major concept here, for it can be both controlling of and controlled by the individual. Career advancement is slowed by the economy and slowed by oneself in order to gain necessary experience. A career needs **time** for daily nurturance to advance both spatially and temporally. Careers are present-held but also future-oriented, looking ahead, looking forward, looking elsewhere, looking beyond. Careers are "cultivated" and "maintained," almost like a garden, where things grow, given enough **time** and care. Plant the seeds now and, in due **time** with **perseverance**, they will take root, but possibly in new geographic locations.

I've heard (but not read) that individuals can switch/change careers anywhere from five to fourteen times in their lifetimes. That made me think, "Does that mean specific jobs or careers? There's a difference between the two." Perhaps the current economic climate, combined with the rapid expansion of technology and the fluid nature of employment, calls for a redefinition, if not a reconceptualization, of "career."

Again, keep in mind that the examples above for coding and themeing were from one small interview transcript excerpt.

The number of codes and their categorization would obviously increase, given a longer interview and/or multiple interviews to analyze. But the same basic principles apply: Codes and themes relegated into patterned and categorized forms are stimuli for good thinking through the analytic memo-writing process on how everything plausibly interrelates. Methodologists vary in the number of recommended final categories that result from analysis, ranging anywhere from three to seven, with traditional grounded theorists prescribing one central or core category from coded work.

Developing Concepts

Before a discussion of grounded theory (a methodological approach to qualitative data analysis), it is first necessary to briefly review two related matters: developing concepts and theory construction. Both of these have been occasionally addressed thus far in the book but now merit a few paragraphs to better guarantee a working knowledge of them.

We progress from the real to the abstract, from the particular to the general, and from the contextual to the transferable when we transcend the "localness" of our study. If categories have been constructed out of the data analysis, put them to what I call the "touch test." If the categories of your study are things that can literally be touched, transform them into conceptual ideas. Concepts are abstractions that have more meaning to life outside the study. For example, *toys* are things that can be touched, but *play* cannot. A *church* can be touched, but not *religion*. And a *politician* can be touched, but not *politics*. As for process codes progressing to social meaning, the specific actions of participants can also be conceptualized to broader or higher-level ideas that take time to occur. A student may be *job searching*, but in the bigger scheme of things she's *career building*. A teacher may be *lecturing*, but he's also *transferring knowledge*. And a lonely adolescent may be *taking drugs*, but he's probably *escaping from*.

When the concepts of your study have been developed from your codes, categories, and/or themes, they become material for the potential construction of theory.

Theory Construction

Not every qualitative research project needs to construct an original theory. In fact, it is quite difficult to do, depending on the scope of the study. We certainly use others' theories for our conceptual frameworks as initial guidance, but it's another matter to persuasively articulate how our own findings generalize to other populations, sites, and times. Some methodologists argue that we cannot claim generalization—that qualitative inquiry is too local and too case specific for a researcher to assert any transferability. But other methodologists recommend that writers leave any assumptions of transfer to the *reader*, who judges whether the specifics of a report have utility for her own practice, or resonance with her own local contexts. In any case, it is important to know a theory's properties to assess their effectiveness when they're formulated and proposed. My personal take on theory development is that it is not the be-all and end-all of qualitative research. It's good when it happens, but it's all right if it doesn't. I would rather read a well-developed key assertion (discussed later in this chapter) about the local contexts of a study, than a weakly constructed or vaguely written theory with questionable transferability.

Sometimes the instruction of theory can get too complicated, so I take an analogous approach to the topic. Did you know that you live with and use theory every day of your life? For example, when you peer through your window to see if it looks like rain outside, and you take your umbrella because you sense you may need it, you're applying theory because you've made a *prediction* of what may happen weather-wise. You can *control* whether you stay dry or get wet if you take (or don't take) certain actions. Your behavior has been *influenced* by something else. When you observe the *process* of foreboding inclement weather (such as a cloudier and darker sky, and the smell of humid air), and it does indeed start raining, you theorize or attribute its *cause* to the particular cloud formations and conditions in the atmosphere. You know that the rain creates potential hazards for driving and even walking, yet it also—in moderation—replenishes the Earth's natural resources. Thus, there are directives or theories for safe *guidance* when it rains, and knowledge that rain can benefit or *improve* the world. Prediction, control, influence, process, causation, guidance, and improvement are just some of the components of what makes a theory.

To use another analogy, most well-known folk proverbs are theories. Some of these classic sayings embody general properties of a theory. The first is that of a statement that, traditionally, *predicts and controls action through an if/then logic*. For example, "A penny saved is a penny earned" implies that you should save money. The if/then logic is: *If* you save small amounts of money occasionally instead of spending them, *then* you will accumulate significant earnings over time. The *prediction* part of the proverb is that earnings will grow *if* money is saved. The *control* portion of the proverb is that we can control and thus better guarantee the future of our economic security *if* we work hard, save money, spend frugally, invest wisely, and so on. Explore the if/then logic and prediction/control implied by these statements: "If you lie down with dogs, you'll wake up with fleas," "Where there's smoke, there's fire," and "Sex sells."

Proverbs' and thus theories' second property can also *explain how and/or why something happens by stating its cause(s)*. The saying, "Out of sight, out of mind" *explains* that the reason we may forget about something is *because* the object is not readily visible. For example, some people may forget to take their daily prescription medication if it is kept in a drawer. But *if* the bottle is kept in plain sight or in a location that's accessed on a regular basis, *then* the person is more likely to remember to take it. Keeping track of upcoming meetings or necessary tasks in our heads is risky for some since memory can falter—we can *predict* that we may forget. But *if* the event or task is written down in a day planner or logged in an electronic calendar, *then* we are more likely to remember what needs to be done *because* we have taken some *control* over the potential problem.

Finally, proverbs' and thus theories' other properties also *provide insights and guidance for improving social life*. Sayings like "Into everyone's life, a little rain must fall," "Every cloud has a silver lining," and "No rain, no rainbows" remind us that, in spite of difficult times, things can and do get better, and we are sometimes made stronger by going through adversity to achieve reward. We can most certainly *predict* that life will be filled with unavoidable minor and major conflicts and tensions, so we can *control* some of the chaos by planning ahead and not getting ourselves into these tight situations. Yet sometimes the *explanations* for *why* these problems occur is simply *because* we didn't anticipate them, and "stuff happens"—a difficult *how* we must accept. So *if* we can see beyond the present problems, *then* we may be able to see future solutions. Thus, these *insights* provide *guidance* for us to endure the trials of daily living by maintaining a positive outlook to *improve our social lives*.

To recap, a theory (as it is traditionally conceived):

- predicts and controls action through an if/then logic
- explains how and/or why something happens by stating its cause(s)
- provides insights and guidance for improving social life

Gibson and Brown (2009, p. 11) also note that a theory can do more than generalize from the particular to other understandings and claims. A good theory can also describe characteristics of the social world, categorize and connect aspects of the social world, compare the social world's features, and interrogate problems and taken-for-granted assumptions.

At its most practical, a theory is an elegant statement that proposes a way of living or working productively. In education, a theory for teachers is: *The more that students are engaged with the content of the lesson, the less management and discipline problems that may occur in the classroom.* In psychotherapy, a practitioner's theory is: *A parent with clinical depression will tend to raise clinically depressed children.* Both of these professionals, equipped with their respective theories, can work more effectively at their jobs when empowered with this knowledge. But note the provisional and conditional language in these statements ("may occur," "tend to"), suggesting that most theories are not always certain but most likely.

Any well-grounded theories or assertions that qualitative researchers can put forth to their disciplinary colleagues and that enhance daily practice or increase awareness and understanding have made significant contributions. But I've observed that what is a sound theoretical proposition to one person may be perceived as a weak statement to another. Like beauty, theory is in the eye of the beholder. I've also observed that some researchers have difficulty articulating their theories clearly or feel that a simple one-word response says it all. I'll ask a colleague, "So, what's your theory?" And he'll reply, "Warm-up!" But "warm-up" is not a theory; "warm-up" is just a word, albeit an important part of what he meant to say. A theory is a *statement* with any necessary narrative to expand on its meaning. Thus, what my colleague should have said is:

> *Life is "warm-up." Virtually everything humans do can be conceived as preparation for something else.* When we wake up in the morning, we're warming up our bodies from sleep. When we shower, groom, eat breakfast, and so on, we're warming up for what the day holds. When we transport ourselves to work or school, we're warming up to our occupation. But even at our occupations, we're warming up for something else: A test is warm-up for a passing course grade, school is warm-up for a degree, graduation is warm-up for a job, each job is a warm-up for promotion, a career is warm-up for retirement, and retirement is warm-up for death. Life is "warm-up."

Grounded Theory

Now that such matters as patterns, codes, categories, concepts, and theory have been reviewed, the analytic discussion can now turn to grounded theory. Recall from Chapter 1 that grounded theory is a methodology—an analytic process of constantly comparing small data units through a series of cumulative coding cycles to achieve abstraction and a range of dimensions to the emergent categories' properties. In other words, you're looking carefully at the small details to get to the bigger picture—a picture composed of a central *idea* (such as "addiction"), its defining or essential elements (one of them being "anxiety"), and their variable qualities (for example, anxiety increases in someone when the addictive substance or opportunity is unavailable, and decreases when it's accessible; increases when the likelihood is high of one's covert addiction being discovered, decreases when the addiction is successfully hidden from others; increases when the addict realizes the immorality of his own self-destructive behaviors, decreases when he denies the addiction as a problem or justifies his actions). Classic grounded theory works toward achieving a *central* or *core* category that conceptually represents what the study is all about by holding all the major categories in place. This central or core category becomes the foundation for generating a theory about the processes observed—a theory grounded in the data or constructed "from the ground up."

Grounded theory is a complex, multistage genre of qualitative research, but an approach that has been utilized in thousands of studies in many disciplines since it was first introduced in the 1960s. However, since that time various methodologists have taken the basic principles of grounded theory's original developers, Barney G. Glaser and Anselm L. Strauss (1967), and created hybrid and streamlined approaches (Charmaz, 2006; Corbin & Strauss, 2008). Thus, it is presumptuous to profile *the* way to conduct a grounded theory study; what is discussed below is just *one* way.

You have already been introduced to the first cycle of grounded theory methodology: the initial coding of data for category development, and reflective analytic memo writing about the researcher's discoveries and insights thus far. Process and in vivo coding are particular features of grounded theory, with the latter tentatively exploring the properties and dimensions of a major category: OUTLOOK. What comes next is the *focusing* of these codes and categories into even tighter and more conceptual categories, with one central or core category identified for the development of a theory. Depending on which methodologist you read, it is recommended that anywhere from ten to thirty interviews be conducted to generate enough data to formulate a grounded theory. To keep this illustration coherent, I will focus on the primary example of the job seeker profiled above, using the six major categories/themes generated thus far, which are:

Career Building
Feeling In-Between
Optimistic Outlook
Pessimistic Outlook
A Career Is Time and Place
A Career Is Perseverance

Five of these six items pass the "touch test"—meaning, they are conceptual in nature and primed for higher-level analytic work. But a **Place** is something that can be touched, so the word needs to be reconceptualized to something that cannot. A thesaurus (an indispensible tool of the trade for qualitative data analysis) offers some intriguing and evocative synonyms to consider such as "status" and "rank." But **Geography** is the word closest to the original category label, so that association will be used to transform the theme into: **A Career Is Time and Geography**.

What happens next is the categorizing of categories—an attempt to get at the essence and essentials of the six items of interest. Some grounded theorists (Glaser, 2005) feel the synthesis should be achieved solely through thinking and narrative; others (Strauss, 1987) recommend displays and models to illustrate their possible integration. I side with the latter to get to the former because I'm a visual thinker and use graphics as a way to stimulate my writing. Bins or containers of various shapes are used to hold the categories, while lines and arrows of various types speculate on their plausible interrelationships. Just one way of visually representing a particular process (not the grounded theory) of career building can be seen in Figure 4.1. It is important to note that the coincidental symmetry of the graphic should not suggest that processes are always neatly ordered. Sometimes they can be quite messy and asymmetrical, and the illustrations should reflect that.

A memo now offers some reflective thoughts on what's been drawn. Notice that *analytic memo writing is also a category-generating method*. It is possible that, through the writing, the central or core

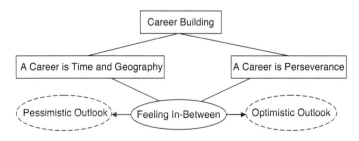

Figure 4.1. A grounded theory model for the Career Building process.

category (a precursor to a grounded theory) that identifies what the study is all about may emerge. Like the memos above, keeping the codes in caps and categories in bolded font as you write better assures their integration into the analytic narrative and scheme:

August 21, 2009

THE CENTRAL/CORE CATEGORY (TENTATIVE):
POSITIONING

At this point in the analysis (additional interviews are needed), I speculate that the central/core category of this study is POSITIONING. A career is POSITIONING oneself for movement through **Time** and into new **Geographies**. **Perseverance** is an attitudinal and action-oriented POSI-TION, yet one's emotional POSITIONS during the early stages of **Career Building** can vary from **Pessimistic** to **Optimistic**—perhaps so reverberative that one feels **In-Between** more at one end than the other on the emotional continuum. POSITIONING also implies that a career is not just a "thing"; it is a perception, a perspective, a point of view, a departure point.

POSITIONING can be horizontal and vertical. Horizontal POSITIONING may be the internal states of an individual's self-perception of where he/she is, career-wise, implying a vertical POSITION of status—both internal and external/literal. One can "ramp up" (to use a popular current phrase) in career but can also slide back down depending on such forces as bad economic health and a lack of personal initiative. POSITION-ING is not just linear, though, and I need to think through later how POSITIONING is more three-dimensional.

As for a grounded theory, I'll put forth at this point (to be confirmed by additional data collection and analysis) that: *A career is perceived and determined by the physical, attitudinal, and emotional positioning of the individual through time.* Still to be explored is how this personal **Agency** within particular **Socio-Economic Conditions** (e.g., a poor job market) inter-relate. I'll also need to check out something I've heard about recently in my communication research class called "positioning theory" to see if I'm just reinventing the wheel or onto something new.

Remember that "Good research is not so much about good methods as much as it is about good thinking." Analytic memos are key opportunities in grounded theory development to think about how your major codes, categories, themes, and concepts weave complexly together. The memo above also acknowledges that the ideas put forth are provisional at this time, subject to revision after additional data collection to test and modify the grounded theory in progress, and after some additional literature reviews of related work.

Grounded theory is not a step-by-step process with specific algorithms to follow. Grounded theory does, however, consist of cumulative coding and categorizing methods with analytic memo writing as a vital heuristic for discovery. Key works in grounded theory and qualitative data analysis (see Chapter 6) will provide more detail on its procedures.

Assertion Development

Educational anthropologist Frederick Erickson (1986) wrote a significant and influential chapter on qualitative methods that outlined heuristics for *assertion development*. Assertions are declarative statements of summative synthesis, supported by confirming evidence from the data, and revised when disconfirming evidence or discrepant cases require modification of the assertions. These summative statements are generated from an interpretive review of the data corpus and then supported and illustrated through narrative vignettes—reconstructed stories from fieldnotes, interview transcripts, or other data sources that provide a vivid profile as part of the evidentiary warrant.

Coding or themeing the data can certainly precede assertion development as a way of gaining intimate familiarity with the data, but Erickson's methods are a more admittedly intuitive yet systematic heuristic for analysis. Erickson promotes *analytic induction*, noted above as exploration of and inferences about the data, based on an examination of the evidence and an accumulation of knowledge.

The goal is not to look for "proof" to support the assertions, but plausibility of inference-laden observations about the local and particular social world under investigation. Erickson admits, in fact, "Conclusive proof is often not possible, especially from data derived from fieldnotes. Yet some lines of interpretation can be shown to be more robust than others. On that admittedly shaky ground must rest the possibility of intellectual integrity and credibility in interpretive research." (p. 155)

Assertion development is the writing of general statements, plus subordinate yet related ones called *subassertions*, and a major statement called a *key assertion* that represents the totality of the data. One also looks for *key linkages* between them, meaning that the key assertion links to its related assertions, which then link to their respective subassertions. Subassertions can include particulars about any discrepant related cases or specify components of their parent assertions.

Below is a sample of data to illustrate assertion development at work. In this fieldnote excerpt, participant observation takes place at a university sports and recreation complex's weight room on a February afternoon (see the Figure 2.1 floor plan diagram in Chapter 2). The male participants are assigned descriptors in place of names (e.g., WORK BOOTS, GOATEE). Observer's comments (OC), in addition to the descriptive detail, are deliberately included as part of the sample. As you read these fieldnotes, think how you would summarize and synthesize the units of action described into statements that identify, "What is happening here and what does it mean?":

The prominent odor in the weight room can be described as "musky, sweaty clothes." The ceiling height is approximately twelve feet and has air conditioning vents to maintain a comfortable temperature, and speakers where rock music from a radio station is playing at a moderate volume.

The east side handweight floor is covered with black, rectangular, rubber mats. The designated area for this observation has three weight benches: metal frames with adjustable, dark red, vinyl or leather padded platforms that can accommodate a person sitting on and/or leaning against them. Benches are spaced to allow people to work by them while others work on them. Weight and accessory racks, holding various sizes and pounds of round metal disks, are located against the east wall and central pillar.

The north wall has large windows providing sunlight to complement the fluorescent lighting. The south wall also has windows with a view of the Center's hall and towel booth. Laminated or plated signs on the east wall state "Weight Room Policies" such as "Collars are Required" and "Repack your Weights."

Prominent on the east side are seven-foot high mirrors extending across the length of the wall.

OC: *It's like a voluntary, contemporary torture chamber; only the serious need apply. With all the metal and glass there's a feeling of coldness, hardness, massiveness in the environment.*

A white twenty-ish man in baggy jeans, a loose white T-shirt, and tan WORK BOOTS is seated on a weight bench. He rises, grips two handweights, one in each hand, and lifts them simultaneously in arm curls. His face clenches in an expression that looks like pain as he raises the weights to neck level. Throughout this exercise he is standing about three feet from and facing the wall length mirror. His medium-length hair is honey blonde.

OC: *His dress is not typical of what most men wear in this weight room. Most wear shorts and athletic shoes. Through his loose fitting clothes and by the size of his forearms I sensed that he was fairly muscular.*

WORK BOOTS is still seated at the bench but the weights are on the floor. He leans back, his hands interlocked behind his head, his legs spread apart. He looks at himself in the mirror. He then looks to the side, breathes in, stretches his arms, stands, and talks to a THIN MAN next to him. WORK BOOTS picks up the same weights as before and continues his arm curls for approximately twenty "reps" (repetitions). Throughout this he looks at himself in the mirror, smiles, then grimaces his face, looks down, then looks at himself in the mirror.

OC: The man thinks he's hot. That classic leaning-back-with-your-arms-behind-your-head-legs-spread-apart pose is just too suggestive of stereotypical male sexuality ("I'm a fuckin' man"). He was checking out his muscles—the breathing in to expand his chest was a personal pleasure sensation to feel himself. The continuous looks and smiles he gives himself in the mirror make him look like an arrogant S.O.B. His self-esteem seems very high and he seems pleased with his own physical appearance.

A fairly large but somewhat muscular man with a GOATEE, green ball cap, grey T-shirt, and blue shorts sits on a weight bench close to WORK BOOTS and arm curls one weight over and behind his head. His feet are not flat on the floor, but on "tiptoe." GOATEE does approximately seven reps with one arm, then switches to another. He, too, faces the mirror but is now approximately ten feet away from it.

OC: The "tiptoe" seemed so out of place—a stereotypical feminine action in juxtaposition with his large body frame. Weight lifting ballet—"masculine dance." Dancers rehearse with mirrors, too.

WORK BOOTS, standing, makes eye contact with himself in the mirror for approximately fifteen seconds. His mouth twitches. He picks up the handweights and continues his reps, continually looking at himself in the mirror as he does so. (Saldaña, 2009, pp. 196–198)

Assertions can be categorized into *low-level* and *high-level inferences*. Low-level inferences address and summarize "what is happening" within the particulars of the field site. High-level inferences extend beyond the particulars to speculate on "what it means" in the more general social scheme of things. Sunstein and Chiseri-Strater (2007) recommend that you pay particular attention to your data on what surprises, intrigues, and disturbs you (p. 106). Using the fieldnote excerpt above, each reader would come to his or her own list of assertions and subassertions, but permit me to note my own. Also, this narrative is based only on a small slice of social action; a more complete data corpus of a longer fieldwork study would be required. The notes below are comparable to an analytic memo—the researcher's private musings before the more formal write-up of the study. For clarity in the narrative, *statements that could be considered assertions are italicized.*

Low-Level Inferences

WORK BOOTS is an outlier of self-esteem in these observations because his interactions with self- and mirror image are overt. His public actions—private interaction with self—transcend modesty and humility. Weightlifting, for him, relates to his self-esteem through the actions themselves. *Increased physical health seems to be of secondary or no concern to him.*

Drawing on my own experiences when I was younger, the actions themselves of working out did not enhance my self-esteem—they were, in fact, time consuming and physically burdensome chores. But *it was the "payoff" of working out—* the muscular physical appearance and the fact that others noticed it—*that enhanced my personal self-esteem.* Any consequent health benefits, like a lower cholesterol level, were secondary. Like WORK BOOTS, I checked my own physical progress in the mirror, too, but did so in the privacy of my own home.

High-Level Inferences

The goal of these activities among university students is to physically improve one's appearance. Some of the physical "pay-offs" of weightlifting are to increase physical strength, muscular size, and body tone (firmness). These men are exercising with arm curls to increase their upper body strength and muscularity of their arms and chests. Repetition of these weightlifting actions increases and enhances strength and appearance.

The more arrogance one has, the closer one stands to a mirror. WORK BOOTS' interactions with his mirror image show a lack of concern over what others may perceive as cockiness or vanity. But I also recall that some have been told since childhood, "When you feel good about yourself, it doesn't matter what other people think of you."

WORK BOOTS appears to receive pleasure from the pain of the activity—"narcissistic masochism" or "macho masochism," if you will. That "pose" described above epitomizes, for me, *men who take pride in their masculinity through hardened, muscular bodies and the physical effort it takes to achieve them. Some men take pleasure at extending the physical limits of endurance.*

The next recommended step is to extract the assertions from the preliminary analytic "memoing" and, as illustrated earlier in Themeing the Data, reorganizing or "cutting and pasting" them into superordinate and subordinate (i.e., assertion and subassertion) outline format to explore their possible linkages and storyline progression. One of them may or may not be labeled as the key assertion—the primary statement that links to other assertions. One such ordering (with slight grammatical revision and modification of the assertions and subassertions, as necessary) might consist of:

Key Assertion: Some men take pride in their masculinity through hardened, muscular bodies and the physical effort it takes to achieve them.

Assertion 1: The goal of weightlifting activities among university students is to physically improve one's appearance.

> *Subassertion 1. a. Some of the physical "payoffs" of weightlifting are to increase physical strength, muscular size, and body tone (firmness).*
>
> *Subassertion 1. b. It was the "payoff" of working out that enhanced my own personal self-esteem.*
>
> *Subassertion 1. c. Increased physical health seems to be of secondary or no concern to some weightlifters.*

Assertion 2: Some men take pleasure at extending the physical limits of endurance.

> *Subassertion 2. a. The more arrogance one has, the closer one stands to a mirror.*
>
> *Subassertion 2. b. WORK BOOTS is an outlier of self-esteem in these observations because his interactions with self and mirror image are overt.*

Assertions are *instantiated* (i.e., supported) by concrete instances of action, whose patterns lead to more general description outside the specific field site. The particular description of action occurs as an analytic narrative—a *vignette* or brief story that gives the reader a sense of being there. It is a reduced yet polished narrative incorporating fieldnotes and participant quotes, when available. The author's interpretive commentary can be interspersed throughout the report, but the assertions should be supported with the *evidentiary warrant*. A vignette based on the fieldnote above might read (and notice how an assertion serves as the first paragraph's topic sentence):

The goal of weightlifting activities among university students is to physically improve one's appearance. Some professions, such as firefighters or police officers, need physical strength to perform their duties. But with most young adult men, the reps of lifting weights in arm curls and chest presses with wall-length mirrors in front of them is not always about personal health or maintaining stamina. It's about looking good, looking toned, looking muscular, looking masculine—and for some arrogant men, looking at themselves in the mirror constantly as they work out.

A mirror can greatly assist some weightlifters to assess their movements for proper execution and safety. But a twenty-something man standing three feet away from a reflection of himself as he smiles and grimaces as he builds his biceps is not necessarily doing it for his heart or cholesterol levels. During a thirty-minute observation in a sweat-odored environment filled with hard textures of rubber, vinyl, leather, metal, and glass, a moderately muscular male dressed in jeans, T-shirt, and work boots—not the typical indoor exercise clothing most often seen in these settings—frequently looked at himself in a seven-foot high wall-length mirror and smiled as he developed his arms and chest in narcissistic, almost masochistic, tests of self-absorbed physical endurance.

I recall a flippant conversation with a female friend of mine who asked me why men did the bravado (read: stupid) things that they do. I replied without hesitation, "Because we *can*."

"Particularizability," or the search for specific and unique dimensions of action at a site, is not intended to filter out trivial excess but to magnify the salient characteristics of local meaning. Although generalizable knowledge serves little purpose in qualitative inquiry since each naturalistic setting will contain its own unique set of social and cultural conditions, there will be some aspects of social action that are plausibly universal or "generic" across settings and perhaps even across time. To work toward this, Erickson advocates that the interpretive researcher look for "concrete universals" by studying actions at a particular site in detail, then comparing those to other sites that have also been studied in detail. The exhibit or display of these generalizable features is to provide a *synoptic* representation, or a view of the whole. What the researcher attempts to uncover is what is both particular and general at the site of interest, preferably from the perspective of the participants. It is from the detailed analysis of actions at a specific site that these universals can be concretely discerned, rather than abstractly constructed as in grounded theory.

To summarize, Coulter and Smith (2009) provide this elegant overview of Erickson's methods of assertion development:

A good interpretivist researcher analyzes evidence as follows: He reads and rereads the body of evidence as a whole; generates preliminary assertions (specific statements of what he believes to be true) by inductive means; warrants each assertion by first assembling all segments of data that confirm the assertion, assembling all the data segments that seem to disconfirm the assertion; examines extreme cases for how they shed light on patterns; weighs the evidence, discarding or redefining assertions that do not stand up to the warranting process; looks for an organization system that links assertions to one another (e.g., hierarchies or processes); for each surviving assertion, constructs a vignette, something like a short story with actors, settings, and an arc that demonstrates the truth of the assertion in narrative form; and frames assertions and vignettes in interpretive commentary, with general and particular data. (p. 587)[1]

Narrative Inquiry

All research reports are stories of one kind or another. But there is yet another approach to qualitative data analysis that intentionally documents the research experience *as* story, in its traditional literary sense. Narrative inquiry plots and story lines the participant's experiences into what might be initially perceived as a fictional short story or novel. But the story is carefully crafted and creatively written to provide readers with an almost omniscient perspective about the participants' worldview.

The transformation of the corpus from database to creative nonfiction ranges from systematic transcript analysis to open-ended literary composition. The narrative, though, should be solidly grounded in and emerge from the data as a plausible rendering of social life. In the verbatim interview transcript below, a teacher explains to an interviewer the struggles young adolescent boys go through when committing to the arts:

> Um, and the guys are even struggling, too. They want to be successful but they can't be too successful, and they wanna do drama but they have to be cool. You know, there's a real struggle, especially with the arts. It's neat to see how, how, which way they'll go. Are they gonna be artsy and commit to it, or are they gonna stay, you know, cool? And even though you know that they have it in 'em, you know, are they gonna do it?

This excerpt serves as a prompt for composing an omniscient narrative of what may be going through a young boy's mind in this situation described by the teacher:

> Jacob had his lines memorized and was nervous but ready to perform in class, as scheduled. He rehearsed his monologue three times last night—twice in front of the mirror. But he worried what Tómas and Eric, his friends, would think if he stepped on stage and acted well. "I'll do it like I don't really care," he thought, "then they'll think I ain't a fag."

The teacher's interview excerpt could also serve as a prompt for composing a narrative of what might be going though *her* mind in this situation:

> As Jacob performed his monologue half-heartedly on stage, Nancy sat in the middle of the darkened auditorium, shook her head and thought, "C'mon, Jake, I *know* you can do better than that." She wrote at the bottom of her assessment sheet for him in the space labeled "Teacher's Notes": "*Commit! Don't just say the lines, create the character.*"

Narrative inquiry representations, like literature, vary in tone, style, and point of view. The common goal, however, is to create an evocative portrait of participants through the aesthetic power of literary form. A story does not always have to have a moral explicitly stated by its author. The reader reflects on personal meanings derived from the piece, and how the specific tale relates to one's self and the social world.

Poetic Inquiry

One form for documenting fieldwork or analytic findings is to strategically truncate interview transcripts, fieldnotes, and other pertinent data into poetic structures. Autoethnography can also employ poetry when it is the most appropriate literary genre for conveying the researcher's impressions. Like coding, poetic constructions capture the essence and essentials of data in a creative, evocative way. The elegance of the format attests to the power of carefully chosen language to represent and convey complex human experience.

In vivo codes (codes based on the actual words used by participants themselves) can provide imagery, symbols, and metaphors for rich category, theme, concept, and assertion development, plus evocative content for arts-based interpretations of the data. Below is a teenage girl's verbatim account of her first years in high school:

> I hated school last year. Freshman year, it was awful, I hated it. And this year's a lot better actually. Um, I don't know why. I guess, over the summer I kind of stopped caring about what

other people thought and cared more about, just, I don't know. It's hard to explain. I found stuff out about myself, and so I went back, and all of a sudden I found out that when I wasn't trying so hard to have people like me and to do what other people wanted, people liked me more. It was kind of strange. Instead of trying to please them all the time, they liked me more when I wasn't trying as hard. And, I don't know, like every-, everybody might, um, people who are just, kind of, friends got closer to me. And people who didn't really know me tried to get to know me. I don't know. (Saldaña, 2009, p. 75)

Poetic inquiry takes note of what words and phrases seem to stand out from the data corpus as rich material for reinterpretation. Using some of the girl's own language, a poetic reconstruction or "found poetry" of the above interview transcript vignette might read:

Freshman year:

> awful,
> hated school…

Over the summer:

> stopped caring about what others thought,
> found stuff out about myself…

This year's better:

> friends got closer,
> tried to know me,
> liked me more…

Don't know why:

> kind of strange,
> hard to explain…

This year's better.

Some researchers also find the genre of poetry to be the most effective way to compose original rather than adapted work that is autoethnographic or reflective of their fieldwork experiences.

A few published works intersperse their more conventional narrative prose with a poetic interlude when a genre shift seems necessary to convey the ideas to readers, or when the researcher feels moved to express insights through another modality:

> Participants expressed the need for more stability in their administrative leadership. The staff felt diffused with the multiple directions their boss took them in, and, lacking a more focused sense of direction, the employees questioned (secretly among themselves) whether their organization's mission statement was being met and even began to question their own value:

No one knows what's going on.

This way, that way,

Do more with less.

Not now—later—

This is top priority.

I wish the boss would realize that *we* are "top priority."

Arts-Based Representation and Presentation

Ethnodrama (also known as performance ethnography, verbatim theatre, and nonfiction playwriting) is the scripting and theatrical staging of qualitative research. Unlike a scholarly article simply read in a "performative" manner while seated behind a table or standing behind a podium, ethnodrama actively reconstructs fieldwork data into monologue and dialogue to resemble a traditionally mounted play for an audience. Most ethnodramas are monologic since interview transcripts of one participant are the most readily accessible for adaptation.

In the excerpt below from the ethnodrama *Street Rat* (Saldaña, Finley, & Finley, 2005), a homeless young adult male, Tigger, talks to a girl who has just arrived at his squat. As he tells his story to the newcomer, he sketches in a drawing pad. Notice the stage directions in italics, describing physical action for the actor to portray the subtexts of his character. The monologue itself was constructed from various interview excerpts with an actual homeless youth, then woven together into a more coherent, self-standing piece for the stage:

> TIGGER: My dad kicked me out when I was just seventeen. When I graduated from high school, he said "Congratulations." Then he gave me two weeks to get out. That was six years ago. When I first left home, I lived in Chicago, in the subway. I did what I had to do to survive. It's all about survival. You either survive or you die. *(he tries erasing his drawing error, but there's no eraser on the pencil; he turns to a new page in the spiral notebook and starts sketching again)* People who live here, the professionals, the fucking little yuppie people, they don't even see this side of life. They don't see it, they're blind to it. That's why they ignore me when I ask them for change. But how am I going to stay fed, other than asking people for money? I hate it. I'm free, but things aren't free. I need things so I have to get money. *(stands)* I want a regular job. When I go job hunting I dress smart, wear button-downs most of the time. If I had a tie, I'd wear it. But, I mean, just look. Who the fuck is going to want some nasty lookin,' dirty lookin,' someone who hasn't taken a shower in God knows how long, handling their food, or ringing them up on a cash register, or whatever? I've got over a hundred goddamn applications out in this city. I've got a voice mail number. Nobody ever calls. I make plans, but anytime I make plans they always fall through. *(sits)* So, I take things day by day, don't make plans too far in the future. Every minute of my life is another minute of my life. *(he messes up his drawing again, rips the page angrily from the notebook, crumples it and throws it; pause. ...)* (pp. 171–172)[2]

The goal of ethnodrama is to use the conventions of theatrical performance (or media) to portray to an audience a live representation of participants' experiences that credibly, vividly, and persuasively informs the spectators. A folk saying among theatre practitioners goes, "A play is life—with all the boring parts taken out." Thus, think of the ethnodramatic analytic and writing processes as extracting the most noteworthy passages from the data corpus and, like a film editor, "editing" the units into a form that creates a unique cultural world. Collaboration with theatre artists better assures that the final staged product with trained actors portraying the participants achieves aesthetic merit.

One common problem most nontheatre researchers encounter when they attempt to "playwright" the data is applying the conventions of traditional research reporting into scripted text. Some feel the need to preface the play with a prologue of conceptual framework explanation. Others feel the need to cite the academic literature within the play script itself as if they were writing a journal article. Still others create a fictional and artificial debate of "talking heads" that examine an issue with no dramatic action moving a story forward. A play is not a journal article—they are two completely different representational and presentational modes of qualitative research.

Dance is also a legitimate mode of representation since, from a postmodern perspective, the body is a central feature in lived experience. Through movements that symbolize the data, the performer physically enacts through abstraction the essential meanings of participants' cultural worlds. Sometimes the dance can be accompanied with spoken text (such as interview transcripts or autoethnographic reflections), sometimes with originally composed music, and sometimes in silence. One of the most stunning moments for me was seeing two female researchers/dancers illustrate the tensions and power issues between an interviewer and participant through their graceful yet athletic choreography.

We often forget that visual images are also texts. Visual artwork as diverse as sketches, portraits, collages, photographs, and even quilts, created by the researcher and/or participants themselves, can be displayed or exhibited, accompanied with explanatory narratives that supplement or enhance the viewer's interpretation. Remember that art is a way of knowing that has an epistemology all its own, and the profound power of images, especially in today's mediated culture, can communicate at symbolic and subliminal levels the meanings of participants' experiences.

Communication through music as a representational and presentational form of ethnographic experience is still in its early stages, for the art form *as* research expression is limited to those few musicians with compositional skills. The field, however, has done some outstanding qualitative work through narrative inquiry of participants' relationship with music and their development as musicians.

Remember that an art form is chosen as a representational and presentational mode for qualitative research because the investigator has determined that it is the most effective medium of the available genres for authentically portraying the documentation of social life. One should not choose to write an ethnodramatic play script or create a visual artwork for novelty's sake or to appear "trendy." One chooses artistic forms because the participants feel they are accessible forums for their perspectives, and the researcher feels they are the best ways to express her findings for an audience.

"Think Display"

Qualitative researchers use not only language but also illustrations to both analyze and display the phenomena and processes at work in the data. Tables, charts, matrices, flow diagrams, and other models help both you and your readers cognitively and conceptually grasp the essence and essentials of your findings. As you've seen thus far, even simple outlining of codes, categories, and assertions is one visual tactic for organizing the scope of the data. Rich text, font, and format features such as italicizing, bolding, capitalizing, indenting, bullet pointing, and so on, provide simple emphasis to selected words and phrases within the longer narrative.

"Think display" was a phrase coined by methodologists Miles and Huberman (1994) to encourage the researcher to think visually as data were collected and analyzed. The magnitude of text can be essentialized into graphics for "at-a-glance" review (see Figure 4.1 in the "Grounded Theory" section). Bins in various shapes and lines of various thicknesses, along with arrows suggesting pathways and direction, render the study as a portrait of action. Bins can include the names of codes, categories, concepts, processes, key participants, and/or groups.

One of my studies explored how the phenomenon of "personal worldview" operated within participants using culture as part of my conceptual framework (see Figure 4.2). I used the familiar concepts of a lens and filter (illustrated in the center of the diagram) that influences and affects how an individual perceives the world.

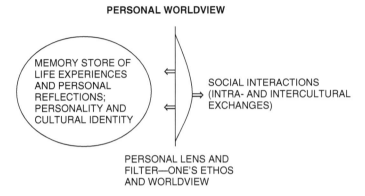

Figure 4.2. A process diagram for Personal Worldview.

To the left of the lens is a bin representing the individual's memories, experiences, reflections, personality, and cultural identity. To the right of the lens are the processes of social interaction within and outside of one's own culture. The directional arrows suggest that the evolutionary process of personal worldview development is not unidirectional but interactive.

Accompanying graphics are not always necessary for a qualitative report. They can be very helpful for the researcher during the analytic stage as a heuristic for exploring how major ideas interrelate, but illustrations are generally included in published work when they will help supplement and clarify complex processes for readers. Photographs of the field setting or the participants (and only with their written permission) also provide evidentiary reality to the write-up and help your readers get a sense of being there.

Credibility and Trustworthiness

After your data analysis and the development of key findings, you may be thinking to yourself, "Did I get it right?" Reliability and validity are terms and constructs of the positivist quantitative paradigm that refer to the replicability and accuracy of measures. But in the qualitative paradigm, other constructs are more appropriate.

Credibility and *trustworthiness* (Lincoln & Guba, 1985) are two factors to consider when collecting and analyzing the data and presenting your findings

Credibility, in literary terms, might be called the unity of the work. In performative terms, credibility might refer to the believability of the actor's presentation. In our qualitative research projects, we need to present a convincing story to our audiences that we "got it right" methodologically. In other words, the amount of time we spent in the field, the number of participants we interviewed, the analytic methods we used, the thinking processes evident to reach our conclusions, and so on, should be "just right" to persuade the reader that we have conducted our jobs soundly. But remember that we can never conclusively "prove" something; we can only, at best, convincingly suggest. Research is an act of persuasion.

Credibility in a qualitative research report can be established through several ways. First, citing the key writers of related works in your literature review is a must. Seasoned researchers will sometimes assess whether a novice has "done her homework" by reviewing the bibliography or references. As an example, one article manuscript I reviewed for a journal purported to be a literature review of multicultural education, but the works of one of the field's premiere scholars, James A. Banks, were completely absent from the report. I recommended to the editor that the submission be rejected and offered to the writer a list of scholars' names to investigate. You needn't list everything that seminal writers have published about a topic, but their names should appear at least once as evidence that you know the field's key figures and their work.

Credibility can also be established by specifying the particular data analytic methods you employed (e.g., "Interview transcripts were taken through two cycles of process coding, resulting in five primary categories"), through corroboration of data analysis with the participants themselves (e.g., "I asked my participants to read and respond to a draft of this report for their confirmation of accuracy and recommendations for revision"), or through your description of how data were triangulated (e.g., "Data sources included interview transcripts, participant observation fieldnotes, and participant response journals to gather multiple perspectives about the phenomenon").

Creativity scholar Sir Ken Robinson is attributed with offering this cautionary advice about making a convincing argument: "Without data, you're just another person with an opinion." Thus, researchers can also support their assertions and findings with relevant, specific evidence by quoting participants directly and/or including fieldnote excerpts from the data corpus. These serve both as illustrative examples for readers and to present more credible testimony of what happened in the field.

Trustworthiness, or providing credibility to the writing, is when we inform the reader of our research processes. Some make the case by stating the duration of fieldwork (e.g., "Seventy-five clock hours were spent in the field"; "The study extended over a twenty-month period"). Others put forth the amounts of data they gathered (e.g., "Twenty-seven individuals were interviewed"; "My fieldnotes totaled approximately 250 pages"). Sometimes trustworthiness is established when we are up-front or confessional with the analytic or ethical dilemmas we encountered (e.g., "It was difficult to watch the participant's teaching effectiveness erode during fieldwork"; "Analysis was stalled until I recoded the entire data corpus with a new perspective.").

The bottom line is that credibility and trustworthiness are matters of researcher *honesty* and *integrity*. Anyone can write that he worked ethically, rigorously, and reflexively, but only the writer will ever know the real truth. There is no shame if something goes wrong with your research. In fact, it is more than likely the rule, not the exception. U.S. President Barack Obama frequently uses the term "transparency" as a goal for his governance, meaning that most matters would not be kept secret but open to the public for scrutiny and accountability. This same concept, also called *auditing*, applies readily to qualitative research. Work and write transparently to achieve credibility and trustworthiness with your readers.

CAQDAS

CAQDAS is an acronym for Computer Assisted Qualitative Data Analysis Software. There are diverse opinions among practitioners in the field about the utility of such specialized software for qualitative data management and analysis. The software, unlike statistical computation, does not actually analyze data for you at higher conceptual levels. Software packages serve as a repository for your data (both textual and visual) that enable you to code them, and they can perform such functions as calculate the number of times a particular word or phrase appears in the data corpus (a particularly useful function for content analysis) and can display selected facets after coding, such as possible interrelationships. Certainly, basic word processing software such as Microsoft Word, Excel, and Access provide utilities that can store and, with some preformatting and strategic entry, organize qualitative data to enable the researcher's analytic review. A few Internet addresses are listed below to explore these CAQDAS packages and obtain demonstration/trial software and tutorials:

- AnSWR: www.cdc.gov/hiv/topics/surveillance/resources/software/answr
- Atlas.ti: www.atlasti.com
- HyperRESEARCH: www.researchware.com
- MAXQDA: www.maxqda.com
- NVivo: www.qsrinternational.com
- QDA Miner: www.provalisresearch.com
- Transana: www.transana.org

Some researchers attest that the software is indispensable for qualitative data management, especially for large-scale studies. Others feel that the learning curve of CAQDAS is too lengthy to be of pragmatic value, especially for small-scale studies. From my own experience, if you have an aptitude for picking up quickly on the scripts of software programs, explore one or more of the packages listed above. If you are a novice to qualitative research, though, I recommend working manually or "by hand" for your first project so you can focus exclusively on the data and not on the software.

Closure

Data analysis is one of the most elusive processes in qualitative research. It's not that there are no models to follow, it's just that each project is contextual and case specific. The unique data you collect from your unique research design must be approached with your unique analytic signature. It truly is a learning-by-doing process, so accept that and leave yourself open to discovery and insight as you carefully scrutinize the data corpus for patterns, categories, themes, concepts, assertions, and possibly new theories.

Analyzing qualitative data is a backstage, behind-the-scenes enterprise. Ultimately, your findings need to be disseminated in one form or another to an audience. The next chapter describes some possible representational and presentational formats, forums, venues, and writing styles for such reportage.

Notes

1. Coulter, Cathy A., and Mary Lee Smith. The construction zone: Literary elements in narrative research. *Educational Researcher 38*(8), pp. 577–590, copyright © 2009 by SAGE Publications. Reprinted by permission of SAGE Publications.
2. Republished with permission of AltaMira Press, from *Ethnodrama: An Anthology of Reality Theatre*, Johnny Saldaña, 2005; permission conveyed through Copyright Clearance Center, Inc.

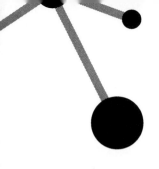

5

WRITING AND PRESENTING QUALITATIVE RESEARCH

THE WRITE-UP of a qualitative research project and its consequent dissemination depend on such factors as the researcher's purpose and the targeted audiences. But most important to consider is *selecting the most appropriate representational and presentational modes* that will best describe and persuade for your readership the core content and analytic outcomes of the study. Like literature, qualitative research and inquiry can be reported in many different forms and formats, ranging from an in-class paper to a thesis or dissertation to a journal article submission, conference session presentation, technological presentation (Internet site, video, etc.), arts-based presentation (performance, exhibit, etc.), and so on.

Literature has multiple and complex genres, elements, and styles. Some of the most familiar genres to us are the short story, essay, novel, poetry, and drama. Add to that the dichotomous and traditional classification of a work as either fiction or nonfiction, plus general tones of writing such as naturalistic, absurdist, tragic, comic, romantic, and so on, and the diversity of possible products are virtually limitless. Chapter 1 introduced you to various genres of qualitative research such as ethnography, grounded theory, phenomenology, and others, plus various styles of writing such as realist, confessional, descriptive, interpretive, and so on. As you've proceeded through your study, research design decisions and analytic outcomes have hopefully offered some guidance as to what your final report might look like. This book cannot address every single permutation of reporting, but it can address some fundamentals of representation and presentation applicable to most genres and styles of qualitative research.

Trusting Your Voice

I always wondered what it meant when my teachers and colleagues told me I was trying to "find my voice" in my early writings. It took awhile, but I finally discovered on my own that "finding" my voice actually meant *trusting* my voice. Trusting your voice does not give you license to publish whatever comes to your head. Good ideas, like good coffee and good tea, need time to brew and steep. Trusting your voice means having confidence in what you write because you have rigorously analyzed and carefully thought through what your data mean. Write initial analytic memos to yourself freely and unabashedly. But as the study progresses, acknowledge that what you write needs to become more accessible to a public readership. And if you are still at a loss for explaining what happened in your study, then have the confidence to say, "I don't have all the answers, but here's what I know thus far."

Writing in the First Person

Assuming a third person stance in your writing does not make your research more objective, nor does it necessarily add more credibility and trustworthiness to your account. A tone such as, "The researcher interviewed ten participants who volunteered for the study," isn't more but less readable than, "I interviewed ten participants who were willing to take part in my project." The latter is conversational, makes you appear more personable, and hopefully makes for a more engaging read. Unless recommended otherwise, write in the first person for your qualitative report.

Elegance and Clarity

One of my biggest mistakes as a beginning researcher was feeling the need to sound "scientific" in my writing. For some reason, I believed that academic and scholarly prose meant using a complex vocabulary woven into long sentences. My reviews of the literature were exhaustive, and I quoted others extensively to support my case. I felt the need to "prove" my assertions by including vast amounts of detail over hundreds of pages. It wasn't until my professional colleagues as peer reviewers of my research bluntly (and, from a few, ruthlessly) told me they were confused by my presentations and pointed out the grave methodological errors in my thinking and thus my writing.

One of my other colleagues, Laura A. McCammon (1992, 1994), was highly praised by jurors for her award-winning work. And after reading it, I understood why. Her research was well-told stories. They included most of the standard elements of qualitative research—the literature review, conceptual framework, major categories, and so on—but she wrote with what one critic called *elegance*. Some think that elegance means "fancy" or "elaborate," but it's quite the opposite. Elegance means *simplicity*. Writing that is elegant relies on trusting the power of the research tale itself, told in a clear and straightforward manner. You needn't try to impress anyone with convoluted prose. It is most often the *ideas* that will make a lasting impact and impression on your reader. It is the rare exception when we feel we must quote something exactly as written, because the writer's way of telling it is better than ours. But what gets quoted and cited by other scholars is one of the highest compliments paid to a researcher.

I facetiously yet honestly advise my students that, when it comes to qualitative reports, "I'd rather read something short and good, rather than long and lousy." Less is more, as the famous design saying goes. Edit, reduce, condense, and distill your work until you feel you've captured the essence and essentials of your study.

Keywords

In this age of electronic searches, relevant keywords in your title and abstract should help your fellow researchers find what they're looking for. This may result in a seemingly boring title to you and others, but the payoff is that your work will be "hit" more often during online searches. A creative yet nebulous title for an article like "In the Middle of the Maelstrom" may sound intriguing but suggests little to a reader about what to expect from the piece. A more descriptive subtitle may clarify the content for audiences, such as: "In the Middle of the Maelstrom: An Ethnography of Employee Tensions in a State Social Service Agency." If you feel that an evocative rather than descriptive title is absolutely necessary for the genre of your work, at least include major keywords about the study in your abstract to assist with online searches. Simply imagine what words or phrases another investigator might type into a search engine field that could access or reference your own study and make sure those words are embedded in your report's front matter.

Front Loading the Findings

I appreciate being told early in a more traditional qualitative report what the "headlines" of the research news are. If you have undertaken a project whose findings include major categories, themes, concepts, a key assertion, or a theory, tell the reader what they are as close to the beginning of the report as possible. The technique frames the audience for what to be aware of as the report is reviewed. Be up front with labeling the major items by using such specific phrases as, "The core category of this grounded theory study is…"; "The three major themes that emerged from my analysis are…"; "The key assertion of this study is…"; and so on. It may appear as if I'm prescribing sterile writing, but these efficient indicators, or cognitive signposts, help immensely when other researchers are conducting literature reviews and wish to build on the findings of your own work.

Analytic Storylining

A plot in dramatic literature is the overall structure of the play. The storyline is the linear sequence of the characters' actions, reactions, and interactions, and episodic events within the plot. Kathy Charmaz (2008) is a masterful writer of process, or what playwrights call *storylining*, in grounded theory. Her analytic narratives include such active processual words and phrases as "it means," "it involves," "it reflects," "when," "then," "by," "shapes," "affects," "happens when," "occurs if," "shifts as," "contributes to," "varies when," "especially if," "is a strategy for," "because," "differs from," "does not…but instead," "subsequently," "consequently," "hence," "thus," and "therefore." Notice how these words and phrases suggest an unfolding of events through time.

Not all qualitative reporting is best told through a linear story-line, and remember that the positivist construction of cause and effect can force limited parameters around detailed descriptions of complex social action. Nevertheless, if there is a story with conditions and consequences to be told from and about your data, explore how the words and phrases quoted above can be integrated into your own written description of what is *happening* to your participants or what is *active* within the phenomenon.

Evidentiary Support

Research is an act of persuasion. Your reader is convinced of your analysis or moved by your artistic rendering of social life if your text presents evidence that "you were there" and that you understood what was happening.

Sometimes, the small details that no one else would be aware of make the case for having been there. But an excessive amount is not needed, just a few revealing ones. For example, a newspaper report on the April 16, 2007, Virginia Tech campus shooting massacre by a disturbed university student recalled the horrific events of the aftermath. One of the most heart-wrenching details I will never forget described the police and paramedics in one classroom of dead bodies, looking for survivors and transporting the corpses outdoors to ambulances. The workers felt slightly alarmed and helpless in the surreal atmosphere as dead students' cell phones kept ringing and ringing, unanswered.

Another tactic for providing evidentiary support is quoting participants verbatim. However, extensive indented quotations can become fatiguing to read, and not every story speaks for itself. Keep the number of quotations to a respectable minimum, and no longer than half a page in length for each one.

Fewer Questions, More Answers

One of my most contested recommendations is my personal appeal for *fewer questions and more answers* in qualitative research writing. I do not refer to the study's initiating central and related research questions, but to a report's closure. Some researchers may pose a series of final, unanswered questions for further inquiry suggested by the study. I take no issue with this. What I find fatiguing is a long series of reflective yet extraneous questions that go unanswered in the report such as, "Why does this problem still exist today? What can we as a society do to solve it? Is it in our nature to be our own worst enemies? Are humans destined to live like this forever?" I advise my students, "Don't pose a question in your final write-up's conclusion if you don't have an answer—or at the very least, a hunch or your best guess. Otherwise, as a reader I'll question back with, 'Why are you asking *me* this? Don't *you* know?'"

Perhaps this need for fewer questions and more answers stems from my action-oriented perspective that sees urgency and immediate need in solving social problems, or from my masculinist yet marginalized status as a gay person of color who feels that quick solutions are necessary for achieving social justice within my lifetime. In the end and at the end, I don't find reading other writer's questions interesting—it's their *answers* I find interesting.

Rich Text Features

Key assertions and theories should be italicized or changed to bold-face for emphasis in a final report. The same advice holds for the first time significant **codes**, **themes**, and **concepts** are addressed. This simple but rich text formatting better guarantees that salient and important ideas do not escape the reader's notice, especially if he or she should be scanning the report to quickly search for major findings. Plus, the tactic is a way of confirming to yourself that your data analysis has reached a stage of synthesis and crystallization. Also, use headings and subheadings frequently throughout a written report. These cognitive signposts help organize the units of your research document, and keep your readers on track with your write-up. Data-based headings and subheadings might consist of major codes, categories, themes, and concept labels, or significant in vivo phrases from participants. Nonprint formats such as Internet sites and CD-ROM files can also explore such cosmetic devices as font size, color, and of course, accompanying graphics or pictorial content for emphasizing what matters.

Formatting

Most readers are already familiar with format manuals published by such organizations as the Modern Language Association (MLA) and the American Psychological Association (APA). Some disciplines like anthropology's American Anthropological Association have also established their own unique formatting standards for publication. Book publishers may or may not specify which format manual they prefer for manuscript submissions, but they may require that writers' final drafts conform to their particular in-house styles and rules.

When I review articles for academic journals, I check carefully to determine if the writer has followed the submission guidelines, including format manual requirements, prescribed by the publication to see if they "know the code." It's a way of telling me the researcher is familiar with the scholarly industry's technical ways of working. It may sound trivial, but I feel that if a writer cannot properly follow directions for form, how can I trust him or her with the content? If class or journal guidelines state that your submissions should adhere to APA format, follow them to the letter (though APA has not yet specified what to do exactly for some arts-based and progressive genres of qualitative research writing and reporting).

Oral Presentations

In-class presentations and conference sessions are opportunities to orally and, in some cases, visually deliver your work to an audience. I offer the following pieces of advice to make these types of presentations more accessible to others. First, don't sit behind a table in front of a group; *stand* in front of them for all to see you. I myself prefer to read aloud from a prewritten text bound in a slim three-ring notebook, especially if there is a strict time limit for my presentation. (Plus, a time limit better guarantees that you will present only the essence and essentials of your study.) Practice delivering your presentation aloud at least twice before the event, and time yourself to insure that you're staying within the parameters of your assigned time block. If you feel you're speaking too fast, your report needs to be edited for length.

I cannot emphasize enough how important it is to honor any assigned time limits for your work. If there are four presenters scheduled during one ninety-minute conference session, and the first and/or second presenter exceeds his/her time limit, it's discourteous and a disservice to the remaining presenters who must speak quickly, or spontaneously reduce the length of their work, to accommodate the remaining time. If there is a chair or coordinator for the session, ask him or her to serve as a strict timekeeper for the event.

Technology can visually supplement and enhance your presentation. Well-designed overhead transparencies or PowerPoint slide projections, progressing at a moderate pace, help bullet point for audiences the main ideas of your research study and can include rich participant quotes. But be prepared for technical glitches by planning ahead. Arrive early to your presentation room, if possible, to become acquainted with the equipment, and to set up and test your visual displays. As an audience member at conference presentations, I appreciate from all presenters a hard copy handout of some type that consists of the paper itself, the PowerPoint slides with room for my personal notes, or, at the very least, a one-page abstract of the report with a selected bibliography and the presenter's name and contact information (mailing address, e-mail address, and phone number) on it for follow-up. Of course, the best visual aid of them all is maintaining eye contact as much as possible with your audience during a presentation.

Styles of Qualitative Research Writing

Now that some of the mechanics and techniques of writing and presentation have been briefly addressed, the chapter now turns to how selected styles of qualitative research writing might read (van Maanen, 1988; Wolcott 1994). Which one(s)—and notice the plural option—you choose for your presentation depends on such factors as your preselected and evolving genre, conceptual framework, epistemology, research questions, data analysis, and intended readership. Based on almost three decades of my own inquiry experiences, a qualitative researcher can and does employ a variety of genres and styles on an as-needed basis with assorted projects. There are many times when these styles blur and intermingle, for one can write both realistically *and* confessionally, or literarily *and* collaboratively, or analytically *and* critically, even within the same sentence. There is also no hierarchy or preference intended by the order in which these styles are profiled. Writing literarily can be just as rigorous as writing analytically.

Writing Descriptively and Realistically

Wolcott's *description* and van Maanen's *realist tale* suggest writing that is factual with "studied neutrality." Although bias-free, objective reportage is virtually impossible, descriptive and realistic accounts remain firmly rooted in the data themselves. No judgment or critique is proffered, only straightforward details of the field site. This style of writing may help the reader imagine the setting more vividly and lend a sense of credibility to the author's experiences—in other words, "I was there, and this is what I saw and heard."

In this ethnographic writing sample based on extensive fieldnotes (Saldaña, 1997), a profile of a lower class, inner-city neighborhood is sketched through descriptive and realistic language. It is placed toward the beginning of the article to provide readers contextual background of the culture surrounding an elementary school:

> Abandoned warehouses and storage yards for construction and machinery parts are scattered within a five block radius of the school. A United Way community center lies directly west and provides residents with immigration information, translation services, and classes in basic job skills and literacy. Directly north is a branch office of a local Hispanic social service agency, *La causa*, which provides credit and loans to those in need. Most houses around the periphery of the school were originally constructed in the 1930s–1940s. The exteriors now exhibit peeling paint and rotted wood. Chain link fences barricade numerous front yards, while German shepherds growl and bark loudly at passers-by. Layers of spray painted graffiti cover trash cans, rusty abandoned cars, and the walls of some unoccupied (and occupied) homes. The three modest churches in the five block radius appear well-kept, but a few decaying houses in the neighborhood have dirt floors and no indoor plumbing or electricity. (p. 28)

Descriptive realism can also precede the analytic section in a report to more solidly ground the data before their meanings are put forth.

Writing Analytically and Formally

Writing *analytically and formally* presents the researcher's systematic procedures and thinking of how the data come together to explain how things work. Descriptions and explanations of such features as research design and methods, including codes, patterns, categories, themes, concepts, assertions, and theories, are spelled out and sometimes self-critiqued for their effectiveness. For lack of a better term, this style is robust *technical* writing because it focuses on the techniques and outcomes of traditional qualitative data analysis. Writing analytically should not be perceived as necessarily dry or sterile, but as potentially thought provoking for readers through its proposed discoveries and insights.

Laura A. McCammon's (1994) doctoral fieldwork explored faculty group dynamics in an educational setting. The title of her article-length report begins with a phrase that crystallizes the primary theme, while the subtitle includes specific, descriptive keywords related to the content: "Teamwork Is Not Just a Word: Factors Disrupting the Development of a Departmental Group of Theatre Teachers."

In the "Method" section, McCammon begins with the purposes of her study, which integrate her earlier discussed conceptual framework—stages of group development:

There were two purposes for this qualitative case study: 1) to chronicle the formation of a teacher workgroup in the performing arts magnet of a high school over the course of a school year, and 2) to determine the organizational factors which affected the four theatre teachers as the group developed. The success or failure of the four sequential stages of group development—orientation, conflict, resolution, and production...—were observed through "focused data collection" or data that were collected through participant observation... (p. 3)

Further into the "Method" section, McCammon describes the specific data collection and analysis processes of her project:

The researcher was in the field 93 days during the 1990–91 school year. Most observations were during 4th and 5th periods, the time set aside by the school for teachers' meetings, conversations between and among teachers, class sessions, rehearsals, performances, and field trips. Field note data [were] coded to determine the frequency of teacher talk and levels of collegiality during each phase…. Assertions were formed concerning the formation, dynamics, and transitions between stages of group development and the role organizational support played in each stage. Confirming and disconfirming evidence…was sought for each assertion through collection and analysis of the over 1,400 pages of fieldnotes, interview data, existing school documents, and previous field work by the researcher…. (p. 4)

In the "Results" section of the report, McCammon starts her narrative by appropriately giving readers the "headlines" (i.e., major findings) of the research news first through a series of clear, explanatory assertions (Erickson, 1986):

The events which occurred during the 1990–91 school year were almost a perfect example of how *not* to build a team. An effective group did not form primarily because the theatre teachers were never thought of or treated as a team. Furthermore, the culture of Valley Vista High School seemed to promote teacher autonomy and noninterference instead of collegiality. Three organizational factors were instrumental in preventing this group from developing effectively. First, no attention was given to building a team during the crucial orientation phase. Second, the extent and limits of the team's authority were never established. Third, the teachers had inadequate training and administrative support. A closer look at the story of the school year demonstrates these organizational factors. (p. 4)

Writing analytically is a litmus test, of sorts, that the researcher has carefully thought through such aspects of data as interaction, interplay, and interrelationships. The challenge of this style is to both distill and detail social complexity in elegant terms.

Writing Confessionally

Writing *confessionally* provides readers with the backstage account of what happened during the study. Such matters as the investigator's personal biases, fieldwork problems, ethical dilemmas, and emotional responses are openly addressed alongside the participants' stories. Autoethnographic work, in which the researcher discloses personal experiences or worldviews, can also be considered confessional.

In the example below from one of my own confessional tales (Saldaña, 1998), I describe the postpresentation period after a study concluded with Barry, an eighteen year-old who had just graduated from high school. This longitudinal case study was a young man I had tracked since he was age five. Barry exhibited during adolescence a passion and talent for acting, and the research presentation was an ethnodrama that showcased Barry portraying himself and his life story on stage. But it wasn't until after the study concluded that I learned of secrets kept hidden from me by him and his family during interviews and fieldwork:

> In January 1998 I reunited with Diane, one of Barry's former teachers, at a local theatre conference. "Did you hear about Barry?" she asked. "No," I replied, inferring that some type of tragedy had occurred, "I haven't seen him for about five months." My last contact with Barry was a month after the [research study was completed]. He was working as a cashier at a bagel and coffee shop near [my university] campus. I was delightfully surprised to meet him there, and Barry told me he was auditioning for a role in a community theatre production later that week. I felt a twinge of irony that [his mother's] prediction of minimum wage jobs for him had come to fruition. When I visited the shop a few days later he was no longer working there.

> Diane updated me on…what she had heard as *rumour:* Barry, still living at home with his parents, was despondent over the break-up between himself and his girlfriend. He was also in

flux about his life and future. A suicide attempt was made followed by extensive hospitalisation. Diane also told me that this was his second attempt (if this was indeed reliable information), the first having occurred during his early adolescence—something Barry and his mother never shared with me.... I was reluctant to telephone him—I have difficulty with awkward situations such as this—but I did mail a greeting card the next day with a message of concern and outreach. I wrote, "I heard you may have been going through a rough time lately," but did not reveal my source. "If this is so, and you'd like to talk, give me a call." At the time of this writing I have not heard back from Barry.

Also ironic was a statement I heard a week later, made by the chairman of [my university's] Human Subjects Review Board at their monthly business meeting: "I'm happy to report that there have been no incidents of adverse effects on participants as a result of research from any studies we approved." Most qualitative methods texts relegate a chapter on ethics to the end of the book, as if it were an obligatory chapter, yet irrelevant to the author's primary discussion on data gathering and analysis. Like those texts, ethical issues in this project did not emerge prominently until the latter stages, but they had been waiting in the wings all along to make their entrance. (pp. 193–194)[1]

(For those concerned about the young man profiled above, as of summer 2010, Barry is alive, on health maintenance for a late diagnosis of bipolar disorder, and working toward a Master's of Divinity degree to become a pastor for the United Methodist Church.)

Rarely is any study perfectly executed, but we needn't burden our readers by describing every single glitch that came our way. Being honest with what we didn't foresee or what may have gone wrong makes us appear more human. I myself resonate with a writer when he or she confesses that selected problems were encountered because I, too, have faced some of those same issues in my own research projects. Confessional tales can also serve as *cautionary* tales and are very useful when they make colleagues aware of potential problems that may occur in future projects of their own. But a confessional tale can also go too far if a writer exploits, rather than explores, the presentation to deal with personal, unresolved issues that may be more appropriate through private journaling or counseling.

Writing Impressionistically

Van Maanen's (1988) *impressionist tales* utilize rich narration and language's power of imagery, metaphors, and evocation to write about the significant, memorable, and rare moments of fieldwork. Vignettes and stories render insight into the researcher's and participants' personalities and their "episodic, complex, and ambivalent realities" (p. 119). Impressionist tales "crack open the culture" of the immediate fieldwork experience so we can learn through the exceptional and dramatic, rather than the typical and mundane.

Harry F. Wolcott's (2002) classic and mesmerizing account of "Brad," a young drifter and high school dropout, profiles their initial relationship as researcher–participant for a case study in educational anthropology, which later evolves into a romantic and sexual relationship. Unfortunately, Brad develops paranoid schizophrenia as time continues, and Harry feels helpless dealing with his mental illness and irrational behavior. Brad leaves unexpectedly one day, leaving Harry heartbroken, but he returns several months later with dangerous, delusional thoughts. Wolcott recalls the events of one tragic evening in descriptive but haunting detail (in the excerpt below, "Norman" refers to Harry's lifetime partner):

> I was the first one home at about 5:30 p.m. on the evening of November 8, 1984. Norman had not yet returned. Nothing seemed amiss as I drove around the house and parked in back. I noticed that the basement light was on, but thought that Norman had forgotten to turn it off, as he frequently did on dark mornings. Only later did I remember that I had checked the basement light myself that day before I exited through the back door. I unlocked the door, then the key-locked deadbolt, and stepped into the house.

> I was struck immediately by two things. The first was the strong smell of stove oil. An oil furnace, fed from a 500-gallon tank on the hillside above, heated the house. My guess, from the looks of things and the overpowering smell of fuel, was

that the furnace had blown up and wreaked the havoc I saw. The second thing that struck me was a 2-by-4, or some similar wood object. I fell to the floor. From behind stepped Brad, hitting and kicking and screaming: "You fucker, I'm going to kill you. I'm going to kill you. I'm going to tie you up and leave you in the house and set the house on fire."

For a moment I could not discern who my attacker was. I asked: "Is that you, Brad? What are you doing this to me for? Why don't you run away, get away from here? This is crazy!"

"I *am* crazy," came his reply. "I'm going to kill you, burn the house down, tie you up. You hate me."

"Why are you doing this? You know I love you. I loved you when you were here and I still love you."

"No you don't, you hate me. I'm going to kill you."

Still on the floor, I defended myself as best I could, but I was in no position to fight off my assailant, who was towering above me and striking me repeatedly. (pp. 73–74)[2]

Harry and his partner escaped and survived the ordeal, and Brad did indeed set the house ablaze and was later arrested and convicted. But Wolcott was forever changed by this traumatic event and its ethics-laden aftermath from some in the research community.

Not every qualitative project has to be as dangerous or life changing as the one described above. I am just as impressed with elegant analytic writing as much as I am with impressionist epiphanies. And, sometimes the most heart-wrenching stories can be those about the smaller things that matter most in our lives.

Writing Interpretively

I was once told by one of my instructors, "*All* research is interpretive." But Wolcott's *interpretation* reaches beyond a particular study to find broader application, meaning, and sense-making dimensions that address the higher-level question, "What is to be made of it all?" A broad array of genres can include interpretation because interpretive writing ranges from theory construction to autoethnography to narrative and arts-based representations. To me, however, interpretation focuses on how the study relates to the researcher's personal experiences in addition to the participants'. Writing interpretively aims for higher or deeper levels of thought—the "big ideas" about the nature of what's been investigated.

It is difficult to find a brief, intact passage that coherently exemplifies writing interpretively, for the act depends on the reader's familiarity with the contents and contexts of a preceding research story. Plus, good interpretation takes time and space to unfold. Instead, what I present below is a weaving of observations taken from the various writings of Harry F. Wolcott (2002) that both relate to the "Brad" case study and capture rich interpretive dimensions. In this passage, Harry reflects on and tries to make sense of how elusive meanings can be, even to qualitative researchers:

> In a professional lifetime devoted to teaching, research, and writing, I know little and understand even less about this case, the one that's affected me the most, and the one that continues to haunt me for answers I doubt I'll ever find.
>
> I felt I knew Brad so well, so intimately, that I would get a straight story—and get the story straight. I was reeling then, and continue to do so to this day, from realizing how little we ever know, heightened in this instance by the feeling that this time, in my own cultural milieu, my own language, and even in my own backyard, I had finally *gotten it right*.
>
> I just wish that it all might have turned out differently.
>
> What is this *really* a study of? The meaning of the story isn't precisely clear because meanings themselves aren't all that apparent or clear. We don't have neat findings, tidy hypotheses, conclusions that can be summarized or reduced to tables and charts. There are no guarantees, no umbrellas or safety nets, no foolproof scientific method to follow.
>
> Fieldwork consists of more than collecting data, something that catapults it beyond simply "being there." And whatever constitutes that elusive "more" makes all the difference. Regardless of outcome, I think the critical test is how deeply

you've felt involved and affected personally. *Provocative*, not *persuasive*.

After years of attending so singularly to the sanctity of methods, I finally realize that only *understanding* matters. We must not only transform our data, we must *transcend* them. *Insight* is our forte! The whole purpose of the enterprise is *revelation*! When you emphasize description, you want your audience to see what you saw. When you emphasize analysis, you want your audience to know what you know. And when you emphasize interpretation, you want your audience to *understand* what you think you yourself have understood.

In the end, we only abandon our studies; we never really complete them. The human condition doesn't remain static long enough for the work to be completed, even for an instant. You need to recognize when to keep reaching, when to focus, and when to stop.

So. How *do* you "conclude" a qualitative study?

You don't. (pp. 209–210)

Since data are not just transformed but transcended, interpretation then becomes not so much a style of writing as much as a *level of understanding*.

Writing Literarily

Some of the *literary* qualitative genres profiled thus far have been narrative inquiry, poetic inquiry, and arts-based representations such as ethnodrama. The researcher becomes a storyteller, in its traditional sense, using the elements and devices of fictional writing to portray real-life participants as "characters" in reflective soliloquy, active storylines, or through poetic renderings. The work can also focus on the researcher him- or herself, thus presenting autoethnographic experiences for readers.

Margarete Sandelowski, Frank Trimble, Elizabeth K. Woodard, and Julie Barroso (2006) collaborated to create a DVD production titled, *Maybe Someday: Voices of HIV-Positive Women*. Interviews and an exhaustive literature review served as source material to develop documentary narrative and composite monologues of HIV-positive women's experiences. In one scene, a narrator's voice-over informs health care workers (one of the intended audiences for the work):

> Some women struggle with issues beyond their HIV status. These include the extra stigma and discrimination connected with being a woman, being a minority woman, and being a mother. Sometimes women are looked down upon because people make assumptions that their illness is related to drug use, prostitution, promiscuity, poverty, or homelessness. (p. 1363)

Maybe Someday profiles how the themes of stigma associated with HIV status influence and affect women's perceptions, as in this monologue, spoken by an actor to an off-camera interviewer:

> WOMAN #4 (African American): People talk about minority this and minority that. Well, let me tell you somethin'. You try bein' a Black woman with HIV and see how far you get. See the men, well, they HIV *victims*. You know, they may face some discrimination, but mostly there's concern and money and support. Then there's the people who caught HIV, you know, because they was doin' somethin' they shouldn't been doin' and got "caught," you know? Yeah, them's mostly minority women, or poor women, or women with too many children, whatever "too many" is. I am sick of that shit! I am physically sick and then I have to handle all that other shit on top of it. It's too much. It's just too much. So what if a HIV person ain't always been good, or maybe is still doin' some of that junk? Sure, a woman needs to change her life if it hurts her and maybe other people, but we have all been hurt by this disease and need to help make things better. But I keep doin' the best I can. Have to. Just have to. Because... my children, you know? You don't know me. No one knows me. But my children... they know me. And I want to keep it that way. (p. 1364)[3]

Some mentors advise that beginning qualitative researchers first learn how to write descriptively and analytically before tackling literary adaptations of the data. Other mentors cultivate an aesthetic approach to research writing from the very start. The license to write literarily thus depends on the guidance and encouragement you receive, and your own comfort level with listening to the artist within yourself.

Writing Critically

Critical writing focuses on the political and social ramifications of fieldwork, with a deliberate focus on the injustices and oppressions of the world ranging from unfair practices at the local level, to atrocities against life at the international level. The goals of both the research and the write-up are to expose inequities through factual information and testimony, to increase awareness among readers about the issues at hand, and to work toward emancipation, balances of power, and the dignity of human rights.

Barbara Ehrenreich's (2001) *Nickel and Dimed: On (Not) Getting By in America*, reports her experiences working at and living on minimum wage jobs for a period of time to learn how the approximately sixty percent of United States workers coped with making less than what The Economic Policy Institute called a decent "living wage." After detailing her account of the challenging environments of selected workplaces and the meager monies she earned, Ehrenreich evaluates the project and presents an analysis and commentary on why things are as they are:

> There seems to be a vicious cycle at work here, making ours not just an economy but a culture of extreme inequality. Corporate decision makers, and even some two-bit entrepreneurs like my boss at The Maids, occupy an economic position miles above that of the underpaid people whose labor they depend on. For reasons that have more to do with class—and often racial—prejudice than with actual experience, they tend to fear and distrust the category of people from which they recruit their workers. Hence the perceived need for repressive management and intrusive measures like drug and personality testing. But these things cost money—$20,000 or more a year for a manager, $100 a pop for a drug test, and so on—and the high cost of repression results in ever more pressure to hold wages down. The larger society seems to be caught

up in a similar cycle: cutting public services for the poor, which are sometimes referred to collectively as the "social wage," while investing ever more heavily in prisons and cops. And in the larger society, too, the cost of repression becomes another factor weighing against the expansion or restoration of needed services. It is a tragic cycle, condemning us to ever deeper inequality, and in the long run, almost no one benefits but the agents of repression themselves.[4]

Critical writing should emerge from sound investigative research, not knee-jerk reactions, personal vendettas, or hidden agendas. But there is nothing wrong with the strategic employment of such literary devices as irony and satire, or emotion-laden tones such as anger, in the narrative. In fact, critical writing demands a sympathetic, empathetic, emotionally engaged, and socially conscious perspective on the world and its people.

Writing Collaboratively

Collaborative writing is a jointly told, polyvocal construction in which the researcher and researched share narrative space equitably, sometimes as a coauthored account. Those with feminist, action research, arts-based, investigative journalist, and critical inquiry approaches may be more inclined to adopt this style. Writing collaboratively is perhaps the most underutilized form in the literature.

Jacquie Kidd's (2009) doctoral research explored the impact of nursing on nurses themselves. Kidd drew from her own background and eighteen others in the profession whom she interviewed to explore the pressures to perform in a rapidly changing health industry. Kidd developed a poem from the data and created a work that "bears witness to our collective story" (p. 317). Only an excerpt from the work is included below:

> *Being a nurse is everything to me.*
> *It feels like home.*
> > *Community expectations…*
> > *accountability*
> > *transparency*
> > *responsibility*
> > *Intense stress levels.*

I just broke down crying
I feel like crap.
Doing nursing work means everything to me.
I thought if I cared enough, then people would care for me.
> *Nursing expectations...*
>> *expertise*
>> *distance*
>> *mastery*
> *I became very depressed and anxious,*
> *suicidal and psychotic.*

This is deeply distressing to me
It hurts too much.
> *Tears, panic, fear,*
> *hiding medication packages and wine bottles,*
> *dread, anxiety, bruises,*
> *comforting food, agonising purging,*
> *isolation, isolation,*
>> *ISOLATION...* (pp. 317–318)

Notice how the poetic inquiry example above is not just a collaboration of people, but also of styles—writing collaboratively *and* literarily. (One could even argue that the poem contains tints of the confessional and critical to it.)

Finally, there is an emergent and niche subfield in qualitative inquiry called *duoethnography* (Norris, 2008) in which two peers collaborate to exchange reflections about a mutually agreed-upon cultural topic. Some of these exchanges may occur through e-mail correspondence/"dialogue" with one responding to another's reflections. The genre can reverberate between the ethnographic and autoethnographic.

Writing the Report – A Checklist

Most beginning researchers will learn their craft and art in a qualitative methods course. A capstone assignment may often consist of a traditional written report (or sometimes a more progressive presentation such as arts-based research) based on a short-term field-work assignment. What follows below is a cursory checklist that summarizes the major components of a study from preparation to write-up, rearranged slightly from the order they were discussed in this book, with some additional considerations. Remember that several elements can be addressed concurrently, and that a decision about or modification to just one of them may also trigger decisions about or modifications to others. This checklist is not intended as a template that must be followed slavishly, since each project has its own unique parameters and content. Its purpose is to summarize and review the fundamentals of most types of qualitative research studies conducted by newcomers to the field. Some of the items below may not be applicable to selected genres, such as narrative inquiry and autoethnography.

Preparation and Design

- **Select the topic of inquiry**, based on disciplinary or social needs, pragmatic parameters, personal passion, opportunity, and/or assignment.
- **Review the related literature** to inform your study about previous research in your topic and for your conceptual framework.
- **Develop a conceptual framework** to drive the epistemological, theoretical, and methodological underpinnings of the research design.
- **Write a statement of purpose** to further narrow the research topic and to identify the main elements of the study.
- **Write a central and related research questions** based on the statement of purpose.
- **Identify the most appropriate participants** for the study who can help answer your research questions.
- **Locate the most appropriate field sites** to observe social action, reaction, and interaction to help answer your research questions.
- **Specify the data collection methods** that will be employed during fieldwork.
- **Propose the data analytic methods** for the study.
- **Propose the representation and presentation modalities** of the project such as genre, style, and format.
- **Speculate on the outcomes** for participants, readership/audiences, and the researcher.
- **Generate a calendar and timeline** for the project's schedule and completion.

- **Secure all necessary permissions and approvals** with institutions and participants to conduct the study.

Fieldwork and Data

- **Insure ethical compliance** during all stages of fieldwork (e.g., treating participants with respect, maintaining confidentiality, exhibiting personal integrity).
- **Collect data** through the proposed methods (e.g., facilitating interviews, conducting participant observation, reviewing documents and artifacts).
- **Manage data** collected through recording storage, transcription, filing, and so on.
- **Analyze data** as fieldwork is conducted (coding, themeing, assertion development, etc.).
- **Revise the original research design** (conceptual framework, purpose of the study, research questions, etc.) on an as-needed basis.
- **Compose preliminary write-up material** through analytic memos, vignettes, poems, rough drafts, and so on.
- **Draw any necessary illustrations** such as diagrams or charts to inform the analysis and presentation.
- **Assess credibility and trustworthiness** through such methods as participant response to preliminary findings, adequate data collection and analysis, and so on.
- **Confirm that fieldwork matters conform to the proposed research genre** (e.g., that data collected are sufficient for developing grounded theory, conducting a content analysis, composing an original narrative).
- **Continue reviewing the related literature** during fieldwork for additional insights.

Representation and Presentation

- **Insure ethical compliance** by maintaining anonymity and using pseudonyms in references to participants and locations in the write-up.

- **Compose the report in an appropriate genre(s)** for the research (e.g., ethnography, case study, action research).
- **Compose the report with appropriate writing styles** for the genre and the study (e.g., descriptively, analytically, confessionally).
- **Organize the report** in an order that best suits its genre and publication/presentation venue (e.g., a traditional outline may consist of such components as an abstract, introduction, conceptual framework, literature review, methodology and methods, analysis of findings, discussion, and references).
- **Revise and proofread drafts of the report** to enhance its technical features (e.g., elegance and clarity, use of keywords and rich text features, proper formatting).
- **Rehearse the presentation**, if given orally.
- **Develop reference material** (hard copy abstracts, bibliographies, contact information, etc.) for distribution to audiences at the presentation.
- **Search for additional forums and venues** for the research study's dissemination (e.g., conferences, print and online journals, Internet sites).

Evaluating Qualitative Research Representation and Presentation

Several items outlined in the checklist above also serve as criteria for evaluating other writers' qualitative research representations and/or presentations available in print, online, and at venues such as conferences, exhibits, and performances. For example, as you read an article you might assess whether the researcher has provided an adequate literature review of related or relevant works. You might also assess whether the data analysis seems to have captured an elegant number of salient categories or intriguing ways of looking at a phenomenon. Or you might assess whether the narrative or artistic rendering of a qualitative experience evokes within you a strong emotional response.

The problem, though, with trying to develop a standardized or even just a recommended set of criteria relevant and applicable to the multiple and various genres, elements, and styles of qualitative research is that only superficial generalities can be constructed, at best. Criteria to assess the merits of a traditional grounded theory study are completely irrelevant for assessing the success of a poem that attempts to capture an individual participant's experience. Plus, evaluation is subjective, even when we try to quantify it. What is novel and new to one person may be mundane and "old hat" to another.

So, how do we evaluate qualitative representation and presentation? I recommend that you do so in context—meaning, attending to your personal and subjective responses to a particular experience. As you read earlier in this chapter, I am not fond of posing questions without accompanying answers, so I will not phrase my guidelines below as inquiries (e.g., "Is the writer's analytic approach to the data rigorous?"). Instead, I offer my openly subjective perspectives on what I believe "good" qualitative research consists of. But even the word "good" is a subjective quality that can be interpreted differently by others, ranging from "satisfactory" to "excellent." Nevertheless, over decades of academic preparation and a scholarly career, I have read or attended thousands of reports, presentations, performances, and the like. I offer nine factors to consider as you experience others' research and reflect on the merits of their work, regardless of form or format, representation or presentation:

- **Engagement**—"Good" qualitative research keeps me intellectually interested and emotionally invested. Whether I'm reading a technical report or listening to a conference paper session, I am intrinsically motivated and attentive to what the author/creator has to share.
- **Clarity**—"Good" qualitative research is written or presented in accessible, elegant, and/or evocative language. It is complex, when necessary, yet told in such a way that enables me to follow and absorb the ideas.
- **Utility**—"Good" qualitative research is unpretentious. The author/creator "keeps it real" by keeping theory to a minimum and emphasizing the pragmatic.
- **Rigor**—"Good" qualitative research persuades me that the author/creator has "done his homework" with a sufficient literature review, time spent with the study, and an exhaustive data analysis.

- **Priorities**—"Good" qualitative research respects, honors, and emphasizes the participants' voices, especially marginalized groups such as people of color and children, when relevant to the study.
- **Unity**—"Good" qualitative research maintains a sense of focus on its primary topic. The representation and presentation modalities chosen are consistent throughout and appropriate for the study.
- **Payoff**—"Good" qualitative research provides me with new knowledge, fresh insights, keen awareness, personal discoveries, and deeper understandings—quite simply, things I didn't know before.
- **Relevance**—"Good" qualitative research, regardless of the presentation's topic or discipline, has some applicability and transferability to my own practice as a researcher or practitioner. I feel that the work has become part of me and even changed me.
- **Respect**—"Good" qualitative research earns my respect for the author/creator because he or she presents the work with scholarly and/or artistic integrity. A reputation is both made and earned and makes me want to experience more of what the writer has published or presented.

Closure

It is virtually impossible to adequately cover every qualitative research genre's writing styles within the limited number of pages accorded to this book. Besides, reading about how to write can only go so far. The best advice I can offer is: to become a better writer of qualitative research, read a lot of it. I have grown immensely in my practice as a scholar by reading a broad spectrum of research reports of various representations and presentations. And, read selected qualitative research studies outside of your subject area. You may learn that you actually have much in common with other academic fields, and your perspective and knowledge bases become much more multidisciplinary.

The next and final chapter of this book offers specific recommendations for additional readings, and available resources for networking with qualitatively oriented colleagues.

Notes

1. Saldaña, Johnny (1998). Ethical issues in an ethnographic performance text: The "dramatic impact" of "juicy stuff." *Research in Drama Education* 3(2), 181–196. Reprinted by permission of the publisher (Taylor & Francis Group, http://www.informaworld.com).

2. Republished with permission of AltaMira Press, from *Sneaky Kid and Its Aftermath: Ethics and Intimacy in Fieldwork*, Harry F. Wolcott, 2002; permission conveyed through Copyright Clearance Center, Inc.

3. Sandelowski, Margarete, Frank Trimble, Elizabeth K. Woodard, and Julie Barroso. From synthesis to script: Transforming qualitative research findings for use in practice. *Qualitative Health Research,* pp. 1363–1364, copyright © 2006 by SAGE Publications. Reprinted by permission of SAGE Publications.

4. Barbara Ehrenreich, "Excerpt from Evaluation," from *Nickel and Dimed: On (Not) Getting By in America*, pp. 212–213. Copyright © 2001 by Barbara Ehrenreich. Reprinted by permission of Henry Holt and Company, LLC.

6

ADDITIONAL READINGS AND RESOURCES IN QUALITATIVE RESEARCH

THIS BOOK has served as a primer, if you will, of the fundamentals of qualitative research, but it is admittedly incomplete. There are vast amounts of literature and resources available to you to learn even more about the methodology and methods only briefly introduced thus far. The best immediate resource is a teacher or mentor already familiar with the field, particularly within your own academic discipline, who can recommend specific college/university courses to take; specific book titles, authors, and journals to access; and major conferences dedicated to your area of study that may feature qualitative research sessions and workshops.

The recommendations I list below come from my personal acquaintance with the literature and the field and represent only a fraction of available titles and resources. Not every genre is represented with an entry; I instead focus on more general references. The major criterion for inclusion is that these works provide introductory, pragmatic guidance for novices to qualitative research. Utility notwithstanding, it is an admittedly subjective compilation from an English-language perspective.

Introductions to Qualitative Research Methods

- Creswell, John W. *Qualitative Inquiry and Research Design: Choosing Among Five Approaches*, second edition. Thousand Oaks, CA: Sage Publications, 2007. This title describes and compares the unique features of five approaches to qualitative inquiry: biography, phenomenology, grounded theory, ethnography, and case study research; includes example articles for each approach.
- Glesne, Corrine. *Becoming Qualitative Researchers: An Introduction*, fourth edition. Boston: Allyn & Bacon, 2011. Glesne's best-selling text provides an excellent overview of the nature and process of qualitative research, including arts-based approaches.
- Lofland, John, David Snow, Leon Anderson, and Lyn H. Lofland. *Analyzing Social Settings: A Guide to Qualitative Observation and Analysis*, fourth edition. Belmont, CA: Wadsworth Publishing, 2006. This classic is a rich and comprehensive "how to" text with highly systematic techniques for conducting qualitative studies and data analysis.
- Morse, Janice M., and Lyn Richards. *Readme First for a User's Guide to Qualitative Methods*, second edition. Thousand Oaks, CA: Sage Publications, 2007. This introduction to the principles of qualitative research illustrates phenomenology, ethnography, and grounded theory. The book includes an accompanying CD-ROM demonstration tutorial for the CAQDAS program, NVivo.
- Wilkinson, David, and Peter Birmingham. *Using Research Instruments: A Guide for Researchers*. London: Routledge, 2003. This handbook is a user-friendly introduction to such research techniques as survey construction, composing interview questions, focus group facilitation, participant observation, content analysis, and so on.

Reference Works in Qualitative Research

- Given, Lisa M., Ed. *The Sage Encyclopedia of Qualitative Research Methods*. Thousand Oaks, CA: Sage Publications, 2008. This two-volume set is a superior reference for summaries of the philosophical and methodological principles of qualitative inquiry.

Selected Genres of Qualitative Research

Ethnography

- Angrosino, Michael V. *Doing Cultural Anthropology: Projects for Ethnographic Data Collection*. Prospect Heights, IL: Waveland Press, 2002. Angrosino's excellent primer on ethnographic data collection includes various exercises and practical projects for individuals and groups.
- Galman, Sally Campbell. *Shane, the Lone Ethnographer: A Beginner's Guide to Ethnography*. Thousand Oaks, CA: AltaMira Press, 2007. This humorous cartoon "novel" is an entertaining overview of a graduate student's journey in learning how to conduct ethnography.
- Hammersley, Martin, and Paul Atkinson. *Ethnography: Principles in Practice*, third edition. London: Routledge, 2007. A classic in the field, Hammersley and Atkinson's text is a sophisticated, rigorous, and comprehensive overview of the ethnographic enterprise.
- McCurdy, David W., James P. Spradley, and Dianna J. Shandy. *The Cultural Experience: Ethnography in Complex Society*, second edition. Long Grove, IL: Waveland Press, 2005. This primer is for undergraduate ethnography courses and provides an overview of ethnographic interviewing and taxonomic/domain development; includes students' sample reports.
- Sunstein, Bonnie Stone, and Elizabeth Chiseri-Strater. *FieldWorking: Reading and Writing Research*, third edition. Boston: Bedford/St. Martin's, 2007. This textbook provides reader-friendly, detailed guidance for small-scale ethnographic studies of cultures and subcultures; includes numerous student writing samples.

Grounded Theory

- Charmaz, Kathy. *Constructing Grounded Theory: A Practical Guide Through Qualitative Analysis*. London: Sage

Publications, 2006. Charmaz's best-selling book is a clear and concise overview of grounded theory methodology from a constructivist's perspective. It adapts and provides an excellent theoretical and explanatory overview of classic procedures developed by Anselm L. Strauss, Juliet Corbin, and Barney G. Glaser.

Phenomenology

- van Manen, Max. *Researching Lived Experience*. New York: State University of New York Press, 1990. This classic focuses on phenomenology and its reporting, plus the purposes of this type of research.

Case Study

- Stake, Robert E. *The Art of Case Study Research*. Thousand Oaks, CA: Sage Publications, 1995. Stake's text is an excellent introduction to the method and takes an artistic approach to profiling the case study.

Narrative Inquiry

- Clandinin, D. Jean, and F. Michael Connelly. *Narrative Inquiry: Experience and Story in Qualitative Research*. San Francisco, CA: Jossey-Bass Publishers, 2000. This text presents straightforward methods of three-dimensional renderings of participants through narrative inquiry.
- Riessman, Catherine Kohler. *Narrative Methods for the Human Sciences*. Thousand Oaks, CA: Sage Publications, 2008. This is not necessarily a "how to" text, but Riessman surveys with examples four major approaches to narrative analysis; contains representative examples about children and adolescents.

Arts-Based Research and Poetic Inquiry

- Knowles, J. Gary, and Ardra L. Cole, eds. *Handbook of the Arts in Qualitative Research: Perspectives, Methodologies, Examples, and Issues*. Thousand Oaks, CA: Sage

Publications, 2008. The handbook contains a rich collection of essays on arts-based research, including theatre, dance, music, visual art, and other forms.

- Leavy, Patricia, Ed. *Method Meets Art: Arts-Based Research Practice*. New York: Guilford Press, 2009. Leavy's superior collection presents chapter overviews of arts-based research techniques with representative samples from the genre.
- Prendergast, Monica, Carl Leggo, and Pauline Sameshima, eds. *Poetic Inquiry: Vibrant Voices in the Social Sciences*. Rotterdam, The Netherlands: Sense Publishers, 2009. The collection features intriguing chapters on the genre divided into three sections: literature-voiced, researcher-voiced, and participant-voiced poems.
- Saldaña, Johnny, Ed. *Ethnodrama: An Anthology of Reality Theatre*. Walnut Creek, CA: AltaMira Press, 2005. The anthology is a collection of nine examples of play scripts developed from qualitative and ethnographic research (interviews, participant observation); includes an extensive bibliography.

Autoethnography

- Chang, Heewon. *Autoethnography as Method*. Walnut Creek, CA: Left Coast Press, 2008. Chang's systematic approach to autoethnographic research includes an excellent overview of cultural concepts and exercises for developing personal stories.

Evaluation Research

- Patton, Michael Quinn. *Qualitative Research & Evaluation Methods*, third edition. Newbury Park, CA: Sage Publications, 2002. Patton's text was originally designed for evaluation research but is now an excellent overview of paradigms, methods, and techniques for observation and interviews; recommended as a comprehensive primer.
- Patton, Michael Quinn. *Utilization Focused Evaluation*, fourth edition. Thousand Oaks, CA: Sage Publications, 2008. This handbook is an exhaustive resource of evaluation methods for programs, in particular.

Action Research

- Fox, Mark, Peter Martin, and Gill Green. *Doing Practitioner Research*. London: Sage Publications, 2007. This text is a superior overview of practitioner research for those in the service and helping professions; provides excellent foundations for clinical and educational research.
- Stringer, Ernest T. *Action Research*, third edition. Thousand Oaks, CA: Sage Publications, 2007. Theoretical and practical matters for working with various groups to promote empowerment and positive change are profiled in Stringer's excellent book.
- Wadsworth, Yoland. *Do It Yourself Social Research*, second edition. St. Leonards, Australia: Allen & Unwin, 1997. Wadsworth's manual is an introductory overview of basic social research principles for community program evaluation.

Elements of Qualitative Research

Interviewing

- Gubrium, Jaber F., and James A. Holstein, eds. *Handbook of Interview Research: Context & Methods*. Thousand Oaks, CA: Sage Publications, 2002. The handbook is a superior collection of chapters on all aspects of interviewing and includes such sections as "Distinctive Respondents," "Technical Issues" (e.g., "Internet Interviewing"), and "Reflection and Representation."
- Kvale, Steinar, and Svend Brinkmann. *InterViews: Learning the Craft of Qualitative Research Interviewing*, second edition. Thousand Oaks, CA: Sage Publications, 2009. This classic presents an overview of detailed interview methods and question construction for qualitative inquiry.
- Mears, Carolyn Lunsford. *Interviewing for Education and Social Science Research: The Gateway Approach*. New York: Palgrave Macmillan, 2009. Mears' straightforward approach to interviewing and analyzing transcript data keeps the researcher solidly grounded in the participant-narrator's lived experiences.
- Roulston, Kathryn. *Reflective Interviewing: A Guide to Theory and Practice*. London: Sage Publications, 2010.

Roulston perceptively and clearly describes the theoretical foundations and their related practices of interviewing participants.

- Rubin, Herbert J., and Irene S. Rubin. *Qualitative Interviewing: The Art of Hearing Data*, second edition. Thousand Oaks, CA: Sage Publications, 2005. Rubin and Rubin's text provides an excellent, detailed overview of designing and conducting interviews; includes numerous examples from the authors' studies.
- Seidman, Irving. *Interviewing as Qualitative Research: A Guide for Researchers in Education and the Social Sciences*, third edition. New York: Teachers College Press, 2006. This book contains specific techniques for conducting an in-depth, three-part set of interviews with adult participants.

Participant Observation

- Adler, Patricia A., and Peter Adler. *Membership Roles in Field Research*. Newbury Park, CA: Sage Publications, 1987. Adler and Adler's classic monograph describes three types of participant observation roles for researchers in field settings.
- DeWalt, Kathleen M., and Billie R. DeWalt. *Participant Observation: A Guide for Fieldworkers*. Walnut Creek, CA: AltaMira Press, 2002. This title is geared toward anthropological studies; the text reviews detailed methods for taking fieldnotes and interviewing participants; includes an excellent chapter on data analysis.
- Emerson, Robert M., Rachel I. Fretz, and Linda L. Shaw. *Writing Ethnographic Fieldnotes*. Chicago: University of Chicago Press, 1995. This classic is a superior overview of the fieldnote-taking process and how it springboards to qualitative analysis and the write-up of the study.
- Spradley, James P. *Participant Observation*. New York: Holt, Rinehart and Winston, 1980. The analytic methods profiled in this classic work are exclusively Spradley's, but several of them have become "standard" to several methodologists.

Artifacts and Material Culture

- Berger, Arthur Asa. *What Objects Mean: An Introduction to Material Culture*. Walnut Creek, CA: Left Coast Press, 2009.

Berger presents elegant and clearly explained approaches (e.g., psychological, anthropological, sociological) to the critical and cultural analysis of artifacts.

Qualitative Data Analysis

- Auerbach, Carl F., and Louise B. Silverstein. *Qualitative Data: An Introduction to Coding and Analysis.* New York: New York University Press, 2003. This user-friendly guide contains systematic procedures for finding "relevant text" in transcripts for pattern and thematic development; very readable with good case examples.
- Gibbs, Graham R. *Analysing Qualitative Data.* London: Sage Publications, 2007. Gibbs' monograph is an overview of fundamental data analytic techniques, with excellent content on narrative analysis and comparative analysis.
- Richards, Lyn. *Handling Qualitative Data: A Practical Guide,* second edition. London: Sage Publications, 2009. The strength of this book is in category construction and factors to consider when synthesizing the various forms of data during analysis and writing.
- Saldaña, Johnny. *The Coding Manual for Qualitative Researchers.* London: Sage Publications, 2009. This manual profiles 29 different methods for coding qualitative data to initiate analysis; includes clear examples, along with ways to develop analytic memos.

Writing—The Styles of Qualitative Research

- Booth, Wayne C., Gregory G. Colomb, and Joseph M. Williams. *The Craft of Research,* third edition. Chicago: University of Chicago Press, 2008. This classic handbook reviews the basics of logic, argumentation, writing, outlining, revising, and crafting the research report.
- Goodall, H. L., Jr. *Writing Qualitative Inquiry: Self, Stories, and Academic Life.* Walnut Creek, CA: Left Coast Press, 2008. Goodall's personable text is an overview of writing qualitatively and for the profession (journals, books, scholarly presentations, etc.).

- van Maanen, John. *Tales of the Field: On Writing Ethnography.* Chicago: University of Chicago Press, 1988. This classic and readable monograph details the realist, confessional, and impressionist tales of ethnographic writing.
- Wolcott, Harry F. *Writing up Qualitative Research*, third edition. Thousand Oaks, CA: Sage Publications, 2009. Wolcott's best-selling book offers practical advice on writing reports clearly and briefly from first draft to publication.
- Woods, Peter. *Successful Writing for Qualitative Researchers*, second edition. London: Routledge, 2006. This text includes numerous examples of qualitative writing, plus excellent strategies for transitioning from data analysis to reporting the findings.

Research with Children and Adolescents

Virtually all methods described in this book can be applied when researching young people, but there are special ethical considerations, fieldwork techniques, age-appropriate data collection methods, and additional interpretive dimensions in these references:

- Freeman, Melissa, and Sandra Mathison. *Researching Children's Experiences.* New York: Guilford Press, 2009. This is a superior, straightforward survey of researching children from a constructivist perspective; includes an array of data-gathering methods with youth.
- Greene, Sheila, and Diana Hogan. *Researching Children's Experience: Approaches and Methods.* London: Sage Publications, 2005. This text includes excellent chapters on qualitative research with children, from interviews to participant observation to arts-based methods.
- Tisdall, Kay, John M. Davis, and Michael Gallagher. *Researching With Children & Young People: Research Design, Methods and Analysis.* London: Sage Publications, 2009. This is a superior collection of methods and case study profiles for designing and conducting research with children; geared toward UK programs but still has relevance for researchers from other countries.

Academic Journals

There are several journal titles with a multi- and interdisciplinary focus on qualitative research, whose articles range from the traditional academic to progressive arts-based approaches:

- *International Review of Qualitative Research*, Left Coast Press
- *Qualitative Inquiry*, Sage Publications
- *Qualitative Research*, Sage Publications

Several disciplines also release journals devoted exclusively to qualitative research within their fields, such as:

- *International Journal of Qualitative Studies in Education*, Taylor & Francis
- *Qualitative Health Research*, Sage Publications
- *Qualitative Research in Psychology*, Routledge

Internet Resources

- One of the best free-access online journals for qualitative researchers is the international *Forum: Qualitative Research* Internet site: www.qualitative-research.net/index.php/fqs/index. The multilingual (English, German, Spanish) peer-reviewed journal includes articles, interviews with leading figures in the field, commentary, and book reviews.
- *The Qualitative Report*, hosted by Nova Southeastern University, is another online journal with a weekly newsletter featuring recent publication links. The site also includes an extensive list of other Internet addresses of organizations devoted to qualitative research: www.nova.edu/ssss/QR/index.html.
- *Methodspace*, hosted by Sage Publications, is a community networking site for researchers from various social science disciplines. Members can join interest groups such as Qualitative Inquiry, Narrative Research, and Performative Social Science: www.methodspace.com.

Associations and Conferences

There are hundreds of professional associations engaged with research. The following five are major organizations that sponsor regular events (at the time of this writing) of particular interest to qualitative researchers:

- The American Educational Research Association's Special Interest Group in Qualitative Research is one of the largest in the organization and in North America. Annual conferences are held throughout the United States and Canada: www.aera.net.
- The International Congress of Qualitative Inquiry is an annual multidisciplinary event with an international presence; the conference is held on the University of Illinois-Urbana campus in the United States: www.icqi.org.
- *The Qualitative Report* of Nova Southeastern University also hosts an annual conference in Fort Lauderdale, Florida; content ranges from seminars to forum discussions in addition to paper presentations: www.nova.edu/ssss/QR/.
- The International Institute of Qualitative Methodology at the University of Alberta in Edmonton, Canada sponsors international conferences, workshops, and classes, with a subdisciplinary focus on health care: www.uofaweb.ualberta.ca/iiqm/.
- The Centre for Qualitative Research at Bournemouth University's School of Health and Social Care, UK, specializes in novel and innovative research methodologies, including performative social science, and hosts a number of annual conferences, workshops, and master classes: www.bournemouth.ac.uk/cqr/index.html.

Closure

The fundamentals of qualitative research profiled in this monograph are just that—the fundamentals of a complex yet intriguing approach to inquiry. Additional readings and coursework in the subject, plus authentic fieldwork projects in which you collect and analyze data, will provide you with experiential knowledge of the field's diverse genres, elements, and styles.

Qualitative research has evolved into a multidisciplinary enterprise, ranging from social science to art form. Yet many instructors of research methods vary in their allegiances, preferences, and prescriptions for how to conduct fieldwork and how to write about it. I myself take a pragmatic stance toward human inquiry and leave myself open to choosing the right tool for the right job. Sometimes a poem says it best; sometimes a data matrix does. Sometimes words say it best; sometimes numbers do. The more well versed you are in the field's eclectic methods of investigation, the better your ability to understand the diverse patterns and complex meanings of social life.

REFERENCES

Adler, P. A., & Adler, P. (1987). *Membership roles in field research.* Newbury Park, CA: Sage.

Angrosino, M. V. (1994). On the bus with Vonnie Lee: Explorations in life history and metaphor. *Journal of Contemporary Ethnography 23*(1), 14–28.

Auerbach, C. F., & Silverstein, L. B. (2003). *Qualitative data: An introduction to coding and analysis.* New York: New York University Press.

Barone, T. E. (1997). Among the chosen: A collaborative educational (auto)biography. *Qualitative Inquiry 3*(2), 222–236.

Barone, T. (2001). *Touching eternity: The enduring outcomes of teaching.* New York: Teachers College Press.

Berg, B. L. (2001). *Qualitative research methods for the social sciences* (4th ed.). Boston: Allyn and Bacon.

Bogdan, R. C., & Biklen, S. K. (2007). *Qualitative research for education: An introduction to theories and methods* (5th ed.). Boston: Pearson Education.

Boyatzis, R. E. (1998). *Transforming qualitative information: Thematic analysis and code development.* Thousand Oaks, CA: Sage.

Canella, G. S., & Perez, M. S. (2009). Power shifting at the speed of light: Critical qualitative research post-disaster. In N. K. Denzin & M. D. Giardina (Eds.), *Qualitative inquiry and social justice* (pp. 165–183). Walnut Creek, CA: Left Coast Press.

Chang, H. (2008). *Autoethnography as method*. Walnut Creek, CA: Left Coast Press.

Charmaz, K. (2002). Qualitative interviewing and grounded theory analysis. In J. F. Gubrium & J. A. Holstein (Eds.), *Handbook of interview research: Context & method* (pp. 675–694). Thousand Oaks, CA: Sage.

Charmaz, K. (2006). *Constructing grounded theory: A practical guide through qualitative analysis*. Thousand Oaks, CA: Sage.

Charmaz, K. (2008). Grounded theory. In J. A. Smith (Ed.), *Qualitative psychology: A practical guide to research methods* (2nd ed.) (pp. 81–110). London: Sage.

Charmaz, K. (2009). The body, identity, and self: Adapting to impairment. In J. M. Morse et al., *Developing grounded theory: The second generation* (pp. 155–191). Walnut Creek, CA: Left Coast Press.

Corbin J., & Strauss, A. (2008). *Basics of qualitative research: Techniques and procedures for developing grounded theory* (3rd ed.). Thousand Oaks, CA: Sage.

Coulter, C. A., & Smith, M. L. (2009). The construction zone: Literary elements in narrative research. *Educational Researcher 38*(8), 577–590.

Davis, C. S., & Ellis, C. (2008). Emergent methods in autoethnographic research: Autoethnographic narrative and the multiethnographic turn. In S. N. Hesse-Biber & P. Leavy (Eds.), *Handbook of emergent methods* (pp. 283–302). New York: Guilford Press.

Denzin, N. (1997). Interpretive ethnography: Ethnographic practices for the 21st century. Thousand Oaks, CA: Sage.

Ehrenreich, B. (2001). *Nickel and dimed: On (not) getting by in America*. New York: Henry Holt and Company.

Erickson, F. (1986). Qualitative methods. In *Research in teaching and learning* (Vol. 2, pp. 75–194). New York: Macmillan.

Erickson, F. (1997). Culture in society and educational practices. In J. A. Banks & C. A. M. Banks (Eds.), *Multicultural education: Issues and perspectives* (3rd ed.) (pp. 32–60). Boston: Allyn and Bacon.

Feldman, M. S. (1995). *Strategies for interpreting qualitative data*. Thousand Oaks, CA: Sage.

Giardina, M. D., & Vaughan, L. H. (2009). Performing pedagogies of hope in post-Katrina America. In N. K. Denzin & M. D. Giardina (Eds.), *Qualitative inquiry and social justice* (pp. 139–164). Walnut Creek, CA: Left Coast Press.

Gibson, W., & Brown, A. (2009). *Working with qualitative data*. Thousand Oaks, CA: Sage.

Glaser, B. G. (2005). *The grounded theory perspective III: Theoretical coding*. Mill Valley, CA: Sociology Press.

Glaser, B. G., & Strauss, A. L. (1967). *The discovery of grounded theory: Strategies for qualitative research*. New York: Aldine de Gruyter.

Gobo, G. (2008). Re-conceptualizing generalization: Old issues in a new frame. In P. Alasuutari, L. Bickman, & J. Brannen (Eds.), *The Sage handbook of social research methods* (pp. 193–213). London: Sage.

Goffman, E. (1959). *The presentation of self in everyday life*. New York: Anchor Books.

Hager, L., Maier, B. J., O'Hara, E., Ott, D., & Saldaña, J. (2000). Theatre teachers' perceptions of Arizona state standards. *Youth Theatre Journal 14*, 64–77.

Kendell, D. (2004). *Sociology in our times: The essentials* (4th ed.). Belmont, CA: Thomson Wadsworth.

Kidd, J. (2009). Fragility exposed: The impact of nursing on mental health. In M. Prendergast, C. Leggo, & P. Sameshima (Eds.), *Poetic inquiry: Vibrant voices in the social sciences* (pp. 317–319). Rotterdam, The Netherlands: Sense Publishers.

LeCompte, M. D., & Preissle, J. (1993). *Ethnography and qualitative design in educational research* (2nd ed.). San Diego, CA: Academic Press.

Lincoln, Y. S., & Guba, E. G. (1985). *Naturalistic inquiry*. Newbury Park, CA: Sage.

Luttrell, W. (2010). Interactive and reflective models of qualitative research design. In W. Luttrell (Ed.), *Qualitative educational research: Readings in reflective methodology and transformative practice* (pp. 159–163). London: Routledge.

McCammon, L. A. (1992). The story of Marty: A case study of teacher burnout. *Youth Theatre Journal 7*(2), 17–22.

McCammon, L. A. (1994). Teamwork is not just a word: Factors disrupting the development of a departmental group of theatre teachers. *Youth Theatre Journal 8*(3), 3–9.

McCurdy, D. W., Spradley, J. P., & Shandy, D. J. (2005). *The cultural experience: Ethnography in complex society* (2nd ed.). Long Grove, IL: Waveland Press.

McIntyre, M. (2009). Home is where the heart is: A reader's theatre. *The International Journal of the Creative Arts in Interdisciplinary Practice*. Retrieved September 15, 2009, from http://www.ijcaip.com/archives/CCAHTE-Journal-7-McIntyre.html

Miles, M. B., & Huberman, A. M. (1994). *Qualitative data analysis* (2nd ed). Thousand Oaks, CA: Sage.

Nathan, R. (2005). *My freshman year: What a professor learned by becoming a student*. New York: Penguin Books.

Norris, J. (2008). Duoethnography. In L. M. Given (Ed.), *The Sage encyclopedia of qualitative research methods* (Vol. 1, pp. 233–236). Thousand Oaks, CA: Sage.

Roberts, K. (2009). *Key concepts in sociology.* New York: Palgrave Macmillan.

Saldaña, J. (1997). "Survival": A white teacher's conception of drama with inner-city Hispanic youth. *Youth Theatre Journal 11*, 25–46.

Saldaña, J. (1998). Ethical issues in an ethnographic performance text: The "dramatic impact" of "juicy stuff." *Research in Drama Education 3*(2), 181–196. [Access http://www.informaworld.com for journal information.]

Saldaña, J. (Ed.). (2005). *Ethnodrama: An anthology of reality theatre.* Walnut Creek, CA: AltaMira Press.

Saldaña, J. (2009). *The coding manual for qualitative researchers.* London: Sage.

Saldaña, J., Finley, S., & Finley, M. (2005). Street rat. In J. Saldaña (Ed.), *Ethnodrama: An anthology of reality theatre* (pp. 139–179). Walnut Creek, CA: AltaMira Press.

Sandelowski, M., Trimble, F., Woodard, E. K., & Barroso, J. (2006). From synthesis to script: Transforming qualitative research findings for use in practice. *Qualitative Health Research 16*(10), 1350–1370.

Saunders, C. M. (2008). Forty seven million strong, weak, wrong, or right: Living without health insurance. *Qualitative Inquiry 14*(4), 528–545.

Shank, G. (2008). Abduction. In L. M. Given (Ed.), *The Sage encyclopedia of qualitative research methods* (pp. 1–2). Thousand Oaks, CA: Sage.

Stake, R. E. (1995). *The art of case study research.* Thousand Oaks, CA: Sage.

Strauss, A. L. (1987). *Qualitative analysis for social scientists.* Cambridge, UK: Cambridge University Press.

Sunstein, B. S., & Chiseri-Strater, E. C. (2007). *FieldWorking: Reading and writing research.* Boston: Bedford/St. Martin's.

Tillmann-Healy, L. M. (1996). A secret life in a culture of thinness: Reflections on body, food, and bulimia. In C. Ellis & A. P. Bochner (Eds.), *Composing ethnography: Alternative forms of qualitative writing* (pp. 76–108). Walnut Creek, CA: AltaMira Press.

van Maanen, J. (1988). *Tales of the field: On writing ethnography.* Chicago: University of Chicago Press.

Winkelman, M. (1994). Cultural shock and adaptation. *Journal of Counseling and Development 73*(2), 121–126.

Wolcott, H. F. (1994). *Transforming qualitative data: Description, analysis, and interpretation.* Thousand Oaks, CA: Sage.

Wolcott, H. F. (2002). *Sneaky kid and its aftermath: Ethics and intimacy in fieldwork*. Walnut Creek, CA: AltaMira Press.

Wolcott, H. F. (2003). *Teachers versus technocrats: An educational innovation in anthropological perspective*. Walnut Creek, CA: AltaMira Press.

Wolcott, H. F. (2009). *Writing up qualitative research* (3rd ed.). Thousand Oaks, CA: Sage.

ABOUT THE AUTHOR

Johnny Saldaña is a Professor in the School of Theatre and Film at Arizona State University's Herberger Institute for Design and the Arts. He is the author of *Longitudinal Qualitative Research: Analyzing Change through Time* (AltaMira Press, 2003), *The Coding Manual for Qualitative Researchers* (Sage Publications, 2009), and the editor of *Ethnodrama: An Anthology of Reality Theatre* (AltaMira Press, 2005).

Mr. Saldaña has published articles in such journals as *Research in Drama Education, Youth Theatre Journal, Research Studies in Music Education, Multicultural Perspectives, Journal of Curriculum and Pedagogy,* and *Qualitative Inquiry.* He has also published chapters on research methods for such titles as *Arts-Based Research in Education, Handbook of the Arts in Qualitative Research, Handbook of Longitudinal Research,* and entries for *The Sage Encyclopedia of Qualitative Research Methods.*

Saldaña's research methods in longitudinal qualitative inquiry, ethnodrama, and qualitative coding have been applied and cited by researchers internationally to explore such diverse topics as:

Education: mathematics education in elementary and middle school, sexuality education, religious education, higher-order thinking in science and social studies classrooms, English language learning (by Mexican immigrants and Korean youth), international university students, adult education in graduate school, Chicago public school teachers, academic careers of scientists, university faculty professional development assessment, vocational education in Australia, women faculty in Australian academia;

Arts: media education, elementary arts education in Canada, music education (U.S., Canada, and New Zealand), community theatre in New Zealand, documentary filmmaking in Singapore, ethnodramatic theory and ethnotheatrical practice (U.S. and Australia);

Human Development: child empathy, gay youth and identity, transgender identity, female African American adolescents, African American biography, teenage and young mothers in the UK, child and family development in the UK, adolescent masculinity in Australia;

Sociology: wives of professional athletes, abused women, domestic violence, military reserve families during wartime, the ethnography of technology, date rape prevention, race relations in Detroit, incarcerated youth in Canada, adolescent leisure in Australian parks;

Business and Government: human resource development, innovation project termination, service encounter interaction strategies, rural displaced worker assistance, open source software adoption, NASA telescope history, European retail barcode systems, souvenir shopping in Switzerland, heritage conservation of England's National Trust, Canadian businesswomen, county administration in Sweden;

Health Care: women with HIV, Alzheimer's disease, spinal cord compression recovery, stroke recovery and rehabilitation, patients living with inoperable cancer, nursing and resiliency, interprofessional collaborative practice among nurses and stakeholders, the health uninsured in California, nursing home care in Canada, renal failure patient support in the Netherlands.

INDEX

Printed in Great Britain
by Amazon